Sally Deam
Apt. B8
1301 Cato Ln.
Sturgis, MI 49091

YOU **THINK** YOU'RE
SO SMART

YOU THINK YOU'RE SO SMART

Jim Kraus

Tyndale House Publishers, Inc.
Carol Stream, Illinois

TYNDALE and Tyndale's quill logo are registered trademarks of Tyndale House Publishers, Inc.

You Think You're So Smart: 52 Weeks of Brain-Teasing Trivia

Trivia collected by Jim Kraus

Designed by Mark Lane

Edited by Bonne Steffen

ISBN-13: 978-0-7394-8340-4

Printed in the United States of America

INTRODUCTION

Ask me important stuff—like how to balance a checkbook, the difference between unicameral and bicameral legislative bodies, and why we have daylight saving time—and I'm lost.

Well, I take that back.

I do know about daylight saving time.

Sort of.

It has something to do with farmers and children walking to school in the dark.

Or the cold.

Or maybe it was both.

Whatever.

> **If it wasn't for trivia, I might not know anything.**

Anyhow, I love trivia. I have been collecting odd bits and pieces of trivia over the years, instead of studying serious stuff. And guess what! They asked me to write a book on trivia. How cool is that? All because I know a whole lot about nothing important.

People have told me over the years that I would make a great contestant on the TV quiz show *Jeopardy!* just like what's-his-name who won a gazillion dollars and made everyone else appear dumber than a koi on a cold day. Here's the lowdown on that. Let's just say I managed to get on *Jeopardy!* I am relatively clever, after all. I have this terrifying image of myself, standing behind that little booth, sweating profusely, looking like a Wisconsin deer in the headlights, flailing at the buzzer, and managing, because of my mumbled, incoherent answers, to go even deeper in debt than I am now.

But seriously . . . wait . . . I don't really get serious in this book. I did, though, have a lot of fun putting it together. A word of caution: If you're doing final research for your doctoral thesis on medieval chord progressions, do not use this book as irrefutable evidence that the medievalists thought chords were what a woodchuck chucked. Seriously . . . there's that word again . . . I have attempted to verify the information presented within—and most of the facts were noted as having appeared in multiple places—but my crack research team—my 9-year-old son—had to go back to the 4th grade just when the manuscript was due.

Anyhow . . . have fun with this book. We've included reproducible quiz pages for your next bridal shower or birthday party. (I hate doing puzzles at a party. It's that "why do a puzzle and prove yourself stupid" thing, when instead you can crumple the puzzle paper up, throw it on the floor with disdain, and only prove yourself rude. Rude is better than stupid any day.)

If you have any questions about any of the questions . . . well, that's a good thing.

As my father used to say, "If you can't fix it with duct tape, or a screwdriver, or a hammer, then it's broke."

That may not apply here, but I thought it was funny.

Good luck and happy trivializing.

JIM KRAUS

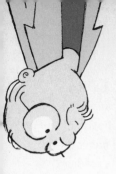

This Week in History: January 2, 1974.
President Richard Nixon signs the federal
law forcing states to set maximum speed
limits of 55 miles per hour.

YOU *THINK* YOU'RE SO SMART

You own stock in a company. It spends more than a boatload of money, maybe two boatloads of money to purchase the naming rights to the local sports stadium. Do you sell the stock because of this dumb decision?

TAKE A GUESS

2

Before they painted that big house on Pennsylvania Avenue white in 1814, what did people call the White House? (It was gray up until that time.)

- O The Mansion
- O The Presidential Palace
- O Gray Walls
- O That big house on Pennsylvania Avenue where the president lives

SO SMART: Nope. Odds are 7 in 10 that the company stock goes up after naming a stadium. Stock experts surmise that the naming indicates to the public that the company plans to be around for a long time. **GUESS:** The Presidential Palace.

TRUE OR FALSE

Neon lights use neon gas.

FOR THE PARTICULARLY BRAINY

The phrase "hocus-pocus" harks back to some medieval magician's parody of the act of:

- O transfiguration
- O transubstantiation
- O transmigration

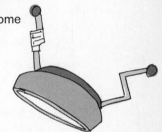

MATCHUPS

Match the person to the price paid for a lock of their hair:

1. Abe Lincoln	A. $9,200
2. King Louis XIV	B. $11,500
3. Mickey Mantle	C. $5,500
4. Beethoven	D. $4,000
5. Napoleon	E. $7,000
6. Marilyn Monroe	F. $7,300

T OR F: It is both true and false, so everyone wins. Red neon lights are powered by neon gas. If you want yellow, you need sodium gas; blue requires mercury gas.
BRAINY: Transubstantiation. The phrase is generally considered to be a corruption of *hoc est enim corpus meum*, meaning "for this is my body," which signifies transubstantiation of the bread and wine into the body and blood of Christ during Communion.
MATCHUPS: 1 D 2 C 3 E 4 F 5 A 6 B.

NOW FOR THE REST OF THE QUESTIONS

1. At the widest part, how many traffic lanes are there on the Santa Ana Freeway in California?

2. If your child is normal, and we'll all agree that he is, how many commercials has he watched in the past 12 months?

3. You're in a hurry. Which drive-thru do you head to—McDonald's or Wendy's?

4. How many fingers are there on the majority of animated cartoon characters?

5. Who in the Bible sold his birthright for a bowl of soup?

6. Name the American company that spends the most on advertising.

7. In 2005, approximately how many pages comprised the tome of U.S. tax codes?

REST OF THE QUESTIONS: 1 26 lanes. **2** In the past 12 months, he has seen a few more than 20,000 advertising messages. **3** If seconds count, go to Wendy's. A survey by fast-food experts reported that the McDonald's drive-thru service took 157 seconds compared to Wendy's 116 seconds. **4** Most cartoon characters are shown with just 3 fingers and a thumb. It takes less time to draw them that way. **5** Esau (Genesis 25:29-34). **6** Procter & Gamble. In 2003, they spent $2.6 billion on all forms. **7** Set aside some marathon reading time if you want to read each one since you need to wade through nearly 5,000 pages.

This Week in History: January 10, 1967.

Massachusetts Republican Edward W. Brooke III

takes office as the first African American in

the U.S. Senate.

YOU *THINK* YOU'RE SO SMART!

In old western movies and television shows, pioneers heading west would arrange the wagons in a circle when they stopped for the night. Is this what really happened or did real pioneers just park them in a straight caravan line on the side of the road?

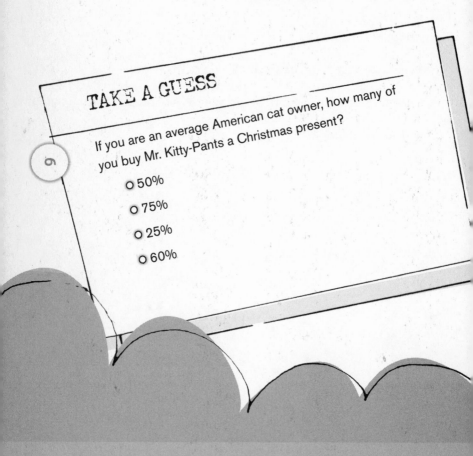

TAKE A GUESS

If you are an average American cat owner, how many of you buy Mr. Kitty-Pants a Christmas present?

- ○ 50%
- ○ 75%
- ○ 25%
- ○ 60%

6

SO SMART: Hollywood got it right—the pioneers did circle the wagons. Not for protection from an Indian attack (the biggest threat on the trail wasn't Indians, but disease), but to create a temporary corral for the horses and assorted livestock. **GUESS:** Over 60% of cat owners in America fess up to buying their cat a Christmas present.

TRUE OR FALSE

Flammable and *inflammable* mean the opposite.

FOR THE PARTICULARLY BRAINY

Who was the first politician to "press the flesh"?

MATCHUPS

Match the Internet ending with the country of origin:

1. .ac	A. Norway
2. .bf	B. Christmas Island
3. .cx	C. Oman
4. .im	D. Ireland
5. .ie	E. Ascension Island
6. .no	F. Isle of Man
7. .om	G. Burkina Faso

T OR F: False. Both words mean "easily set on fire." The opposite is *nonflammable*.
BRAINY: Thomas Jefferson was the first president to actually shake hands with people. Before then, most people, presidents included, offered a slight, dignified bow. **MATCH-UPS:** 1 E 2 G 3 B 4 F 5 D 6 A 7 C.

NOW FOR THE REST OF THE QUESTIONS

1. How many Ringling brothers were in the Ringling Brothers Circus? Can you name any of them?

2. What famous politician had a close relationship with fast food?

3. What key ingredient in crayons causes that wonderfully delicious smell when you open the box?

4. Who planted the first garden?

5. Who held the first American patent?

6. Who was the last U.S. president to keep a cow tethered on the lawn at the White House?

7. What baseball player–turned–evangelist became famous in the early part of the 20th century for his theatrics and anti-liquor sermons?

REST OF THE QUESTIONS: 1 Seven: Al, Gus, Otto, Alf, Charles, John, Henry. They also had a sister, Ida. **2** Thomas Jefferson. He was the man who coined the term "french fries." He described the fried delicacy as "potatoes fried in the French manner." I think that's why Ronald McDonald speaks with the hint of a French accent. **3** Vegetarians, be forewarned: It's beef fat. **4** God (Genesis 2:8). **5** Samuel Hopkins. In 1790, Hopkins was given patent #1 for a new process of making potash. The patent was signed by George Washington. **6** William Howard Taft, who was president from 1909 through 1913. **7** Billy Sunday.

This Week in History: January 17, 1949. The first VW Beetle arrives in the United States from Germany. The distinctly shaped Volkswagen—the "people's car"—was designed by Ferdinand Porsche.

9

YOU *THINK* YOU'RE SO SMART!

You are an average American consumer, consuming the average amount of average stuff that gets consumed on the average day. So how much garbage, on average, do you throw out each and every day?

TAKE A GUESS

10

How many M&M colors are there?

- ○ 6
- ○ 8
- ○ 12
- ○ 18
- ○ 21

SO SMART: The average American discards 5 pounds of waste each and every day, a combination of actual garbage and recyclable materials. **GUESS:** You get credit for 6 and 21, since both are true. The commonly-found 6 colors are red, orange, yellow, green, blue, and brown. However, there are 21 M&M total colors available, with the other colors used for special holiday bags and promotional offerings.

TRUE OR FALSE

To get to the Klondike, you go to Alaska first.

FOR THE PARTICULARLY BRAINY

How small of a hole can a cat squeeze through?

MATCHUPS

Match these 2- and 3-time Nobel Prize winners to their categories:

1. Marie Curie
2. Linus Pauling
3. UN High Commission for Refugees
4. The Red Cross
5. Frederick Sanger
6. John Bardeen

A. Physics and Physics
B. Chemistry and Peace
C. Peace, Peace, and Peace
D. Peace and Peace
E. Physics and Chemistry
F. Chemistry and Chemistry

NOW FOR THE REST OF THE QUESTIONS

1. How many languages would you need to know to speak to every New York City cabbie in his or her native language?

2. These days, the "Wicked" Bible could possibly make it to the best seller list. What was the "Wicked" Bible?

3. The famous "monkey trial" was held in 1925 in Dayton, Tennessee. What was the controversial subject of that trial?

4. Why should we all be grateful to Horace Wells?

5. What are camel's hair paintbrushes made from?

6. With all those big red "Top Secret" stamps, how many government workers actually have the authority to classify something as secret?

7. If you have always wanted to live in a log cabin, what state is the best spot for your dream home?

12

REST OF THE QUESTIONS: 1 New York cabbies speak at least 90 different languages. **2** A 1632 English Bible that omitted the word *not* in the 7th commandment; thus reading, "Thou shalt commit adultery." **3** Evolution. The trial was also known as the "Scopes Trial"—the defendant, John Scopes, was a high school science teacher accused of teaching evolution as fact. **4** He invented dental anesthesia in 1844. **5** You guessed it—squirrel hair! **6** A lot of red ink is being ordered for the 4,000 government workers who have a big "Top Secret" stamp in their desk drawer. **7** Maine, because log cabins are exempt from property taxes.

This Week in History: January 24, 1984.

The first Macintosh computers go on sale.

The price? A cool $2,495 each.

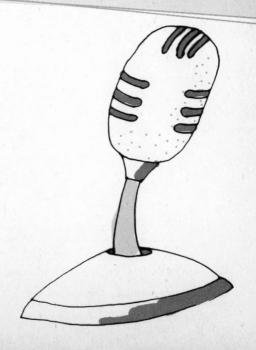

YOU *THINK* YOU'RE SO SMART!

Did Vincent van Gogh once cut off his ear to impress his girlfriend?

TAKE A GUESS

What toy was the first one to be mass-produced in the United States?

- O marbles
- O checkers
- O a chess set
- O jump rope

SO SMART: Well, sort of. Both a *yes* or *no* receive partial credit. Van Gogh did do some cutting, slicing off a small portion of his left ear lobe. It's still very creepy, but at least he didn't whack the whole thing off. **GUESS:** You get all the marbles if that was your answer. All the toys listed were 19th-century favorites, of course, but clay marbles were mass-produced in the United States starting in 1884. The rest of the toys were produced 1 order at a time.

TRUE OR FALSE

Eating late at night will make you fat.

FOR THE PARTICULARLY BRAINY

What metal—gold, silver, tin, copper, iron, mercury, or lead—is not mentioned in the Bible?

MATCHUPS

Match these working titles with their published book titles:

1. *Catch-18*

A. *War and Peace*

2. *Pansy*

B. *The Great Gatsby*

3. *1805*

C. *Gone with the Wind*

4. *Trimalchio in West Egg*

D. *Catch-22*

5. *The Last Man in Europe*

E. *1984*

T OR F: False. It doesn't matter when you eat it; calories are calories. What makes some people gain weight with late-night snacking is the sort of food they eat at night—chips, ice cream, candy, fast-food menu items, and the like. **BRAINY:** Mercury.

MATCHUPS: 1 D 2 C 3 A 4 B 5 E.

NOW FOR THE REST OF THE QUESTIONS

1. You become a major league baseball player by working very, very hard. You get signed by the Yankees. When the team owner asks you what number you'd like on your jersey, you say "42." "Sorry, kid," he answers. "No can do." Why can't he?

2. How many years after the pencil was invented did someone finally think of an eraser to top it off?

3. How far does the average shopping cart travel before being turned into scrap metal?

4. Who buys the most kosher food in America?

5. When Joshua and his army were fighting the Amorites, what weather phenomenon did God use to convincingly defeat the Israelites' enemy?

6. Which city is farther west—Reno, Nevada, or Los Angeles, California? (No fair looking at a map.)

7. True or False: Daniel Webster's best-selling book was his dictionary.

REST OF THE QUESTIONS: 1 In 1997, every major league team simultaneously retired number 42—worn by Jackie Robinson during his career with the Brooklyn Dodgers. **2** The eraser met the pencil 220 years after the pencil made its debut. **3** A mere 30,000 miles—without an oil change! **4** Ha! It's not Jews—they consume only 20% of all the kosher food produced in the United States. Since "kosher" clearly delineates between items containing milk and meat, Muslims, Seventh-Day Adventists, vegetarians, and lactose-intolerant people make up the bulk of kosher food purchasers. **5** A terrible hailstorm (Joshua 10:6-11). **6** Bet you could've guessed that it's Reno, Nevada. **7 False.** His best seller, published in 1783, was the the *American Spelling Book*, nicknamed the "Blue-Backed Speller." He sold over a million copies during his lifetime. But the book's popularity didn't die with Webster—the book never went out of print. Today it is estimated that more than 100 million copies have helped spellers achieve perfection.

This Week in History: January 30, 1933.

With the stirring music of the *William Tell*

Overture and a definitive "Hi-Yo, Silver!

Away!" the Lone Ranger makes his debut on

Detroit's WXYZ radio station.

YOU *THINK* YOU'RE SO SMART!

The daddy longlegs is the largest spider, correct?

TAKE A GUESS

A fast runner can outrun a grizzly.

○ yes

○ no

○ for a short distance, maybe

18

SO SMART: False. Although a daddy longlegs resembles a spider, it is classified with scorpions and ticks. It is also called "harvestman." **GUESS:** Sorry, no; you're bear bait. Bears have been timed at 44 feet per second. A record-breaking Olympic sprinter is only able to run about 33 feet per second.

TRUE OR FALSE

The world's largest wooden plane, the *Spruce Goose*, built by Howard Hughes, is made out of spruce.

FOR THE PARTICULARLY BRAINY

What did Mr. Potato Head used to do that he doesn't do any more?

MATCHUPS

You've probably said, "Cheese," to coax smiles from a group of people you're photographing. What do photographers in other countries say in their native tongues to coax the broadest grins?

1. Korea	A. Omelet
2. Japan	B. Fax
3. Spain	C. Whiskey
4. Czech Republic	D. Kimchi (pickled cabbage)
5. China	E. Qiezi (eggplant)
6. Sweden	F. Patata (potato)

T OR F: False. The plane was almost entirely constructed from birch laminate. Howard Hughes designated the flying boat as *H-4*, and he despised its popular nickname, the *Spruce Goose*. **BRAINY:** He used to smoke a pipe. Surgeon General C. Everett Koop lobbied Hasbro to eliminate it, saying it was a bad example to kids. In 1987, the pipe was retired. When the toy was first introduced in 1952, all the parts came stuck on a piece of Styrofoam and you actually had to use a real potato for the body to make it all work. **MATCHUPS: 1** D **2** C **3** F **4** B **5** E **6** A.

NOW FOR THE REST OF THE QUESTIONS

1. I have a pristine Rubik's Cube (I never bothered twisting it). How many solutions or correct alignments are there for the cube of many colors?

2. As of November 2006, golf tees came in how many different flavors?

3. Besides being a television pioneer and Lucy's husband, what else made Desi Arnaz Jr. famous?

4. Starbucks has been around for a while now. But when *was* the world's first coffee shop opened?

5. What's the ratio of men lefties to women lefties?

6. What grief-stricken woman in the Bible turned away from her diseased husband because his breath was so offensive?

7. Andrew Carnegie may have been a strike buster and a steel baron, but he did build a lot of libraries. How many libraries in the United States owe their existence to Mr. Carnegie?

REST OF THE QUESTIONS: 1 Just 1. **2** The company Tasty Tees makes 4 flavors for golf tees—grape, cherry, mega-mint, and strawberry. I guess if you wanted to be technical, you could say "plain wood" is a flavor, too. **3** He appeared on the first cover of *TV Guide*, which up until the advent of cable television, was the most widely read magazine in America. **4** In 1475, coffee drinkers were hanging out together in Constantinople. **5** There are 2 left-handed men to every 1 left-handed woman. **6** Job's wife (Job 19:17). **7** Carnegie gave away nearly $60 million to build 2,509 libraries. He once said, "To die rich is to die disgraced."

This Week in History: February 9, 1964.
The British rock-and-roll invasion begins as
the Beatles appear live on the *Ed Sullivan
Show*. The show's live audience of 728 people,
the majority of them screaming girls, were
treated to 5 songs, including "All My
Lovin'" and "She Loves You."

YOU *THINK* YOU'RE SO SMART!

You've met a wonderful woman and everything is going along swimmingly, except that her cat hates you. It's obvious that the cat thinks you're evil and is trying his furry best to get rid of you. What are the odds of your perfect woman ending your promising romantic relationship because of her precious tabby?

TAKE A GUESS

22

How often does the word *Bible* appear in the Bible?

O Once in the New Testament

O 20 times in the Bible

O Never

TRUE OR FALSE

The average American person chews 300 sticks of gum every year.

FOR THE PARTICULARLY BRAINY

Who was the first U.S. presidential candidate who sponsored and ran a television ad campaign during his run for the White House?

MATCHUPS

Match these phrases with the correct NKJV Bible reference:

23

1. Pearls before swine
2. Signs of the times
3. Fat of the land
4. The truth shall make you free
5. How the mighty have fallen
6. Out of the mouth of babes
7. Skin of my teeth
8. Stranger in a strange land

A. 2 Samuel 1:25

B. Job 19:20

C. Exodus 2:22

D. Matthew 16:3

E. Psalm 8:2

F. Matthew 7:6

G. John 8:32

H. Genesis 45:18

NOW FOR THE REST OF THE QUESTIONS

1. What does "ETAISONHRDLUCMFWYPGVBKJQXZ" represent?

2. What country has more English speakers, China or the United States?

3. What does the name *Kodak* stand for?

4. God says we should all rest on Sunday, right?

5. If you are the average Snickers bar, how many nuts are hiding in your caramel-nougat?

6. You probably have one in your refrigerator right now: a gallon of milk in a plastic container. Nearly all of these containers have a dimple or a sunken-in area on the sides. Why?

7. This biblical strongman invented a very formidable weapon. Who slew 1,000 men with the jawbone of an ass?

24

This Week in History: February 14, 1978.

Texas Instruments patents the first

microchip.

YOU *THINK* YOU'RE SO SMART **!**

You're in a store. The salesperson pulls out a Brannock device. Should you run?

TAKE A GUESS

26

Which is easier: hitting a hole in one in golf or bowling a perfect 300 game?

TRUE OR FALSE

The average American 3-year-old recognizes at least 100 brand names or company logos.

FOR THE PARTICULARLY BRAINY

If you're really lost, you can get a general sense of what direction you're headed if you know the route number of the highway. What's the special code? (Of course, if you are out in the middle of nowhere with no highway markers, forget it.)

MATCHUPS

Match the person to their tattoo:

1. Winston Churchill   A. Family crest

2. Joseph Stalin   B. Death's head

3. Franklin Roosevelt   C. Anchor

4. Ashlee Simpson   D. Angels

5. Tim Duncan   E. The word *Love*

6. Drew Barrymore   F. Jester

T OR F: The answer is true, unfortunately. At the age of 2, my son surprised my wife and me by pointing out McDonald's—just barely moments after he figured out how to say "mama." **BRAINY:** Odd-numbered highways go north and south. Even-numbered highways go east and west. Highways with 1- and 2-digit numbers are through routes. 3-digit routes that begin with an even number are usually beltways around a city. 3-digit routes that begin with an odd number are spur routes into a city. **MATCHUPS:** 1 C
2 B 3 A 4 E 5 F 6 D.

NOW FOR THE REST
OF THE QUESTIONS

1. If you were an average farmer in 1910, how many acres did you farm?

2. If you are a farmer today, how big is your farm?

3. Within a million, how many Americans call themselves fishermen?

4. What American county names are the most duplicated? We've listed the top 11 answers. (Hint: If you know your presidents, you'll get more than half.)

5. What is the attention span of the average American student?

6. Who receives the most Valentine cards?

7. What Bible prophet was married to a Bible prophet?

REST OF THE QUESTIONS: 1 140 acres. 2 Over 450 acres. 3 A whopping 34 million. 4 In descending order, the most often used names are: Washington, Jefferson, Franklin, Jackson, Lincoln, Madison, Montgomery, Union, Clay, Marion, and Monroe. 5 20 minutes. 6 Schoolteachers get the most, followed by children, mothers, wives, and sweethearts. 7 Isaiah, whose wife was called a prophetess (8:3).

This Week in History: February 20, 1962. John Glenn makes the first American orbital space flight, flying in the *Friendship* 7 Mercury capsule. He circles the earth 3 times before safely landing in water near the Bahamas.

29

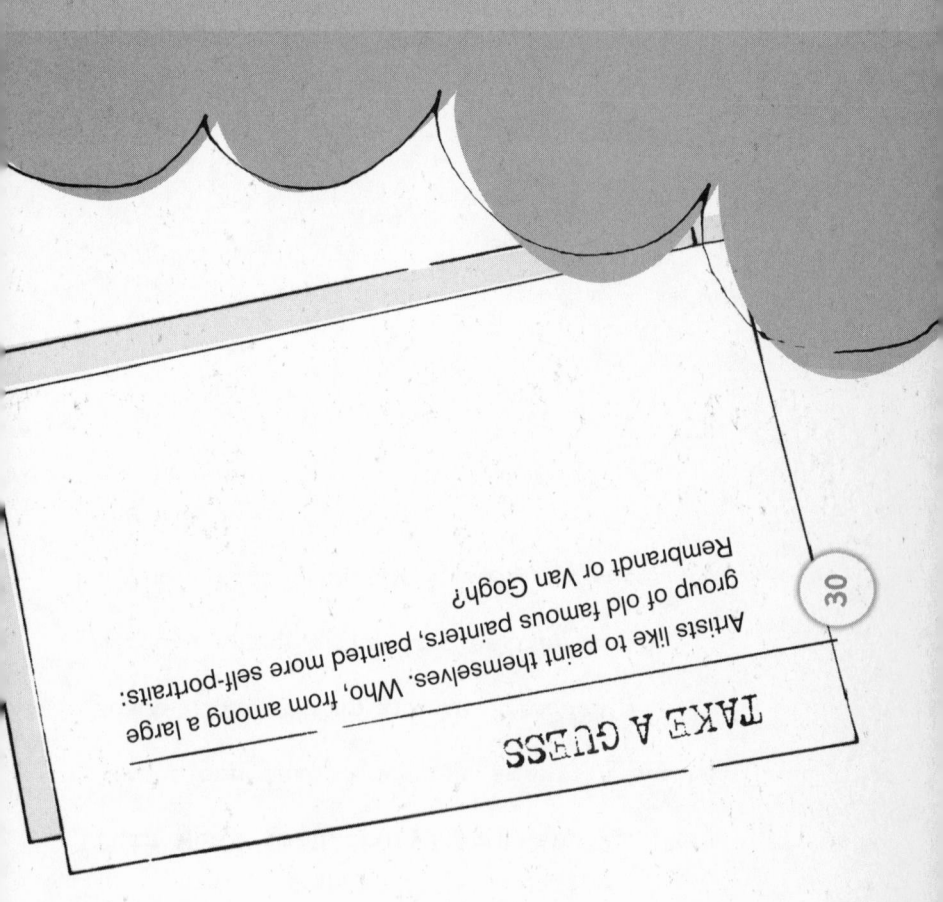

TAKE A GUESS

Artists like to paint themselves. Who, from among a large group of old famous painters, painted more self-portraits: Rembrandt or Van Gogh?

30

YOU THINK YOU'RE SO SMART

If you enter a store 100 times, how many of those times did you turn to the right once inside the store?

TRUE OR FALSE

You're expecting a baby. Congratulations! The doctor says the baby is due March 1. You can trust his calculations—right?

FOR THE PARTICULARLY BRAINY

If you like living on the edge, what might be your favorite—though potentially deadly—entrée?

MATCHUPS

Match the percentage of each genre of book in print as of December 2006:

31

1. Romance novels   A. 8%

2. Mysteries or thrillers   B. 35%

3. Science fiction   C. 20%

T OR F: False. If he's the average doctor, he will not have a good winning percentage. Only 1 baby in 40 arrives on the due date. And twice as many babies are born after the due date as are born before it. **BRAINY:** Fugu, better known as the puffer fish, is served as a delicacy in Japanese sushi bars, but can be deadly if prepared incorrectly. To date, more than 200 people have died in Japan by eating bad fugu. **MATCHUPS:**

NOW FOR THE REST OF THE QUESTIONS

1. Why are the San Diego Chargers called the Chargers?

2. If you have 4 pencils, how many are yellow?

3. Which charity raises the most money every year?

4. What is the only letter of the alphabet that does not appear in the name of any state?

5. What is the longest verse in the Bible?

6. Johann Wolfgang Goethe wrote *Faust*–and had a special edition printed in 1867. What was special about it?

7. What U.S. city is the most misspelled?

32

This Week in History: February 28, 1982. After nearly a decade of legal maneuvering, the J. Paul Getty Museum in California receives a $1.2 billion bequest from its late founder. It is now the most richly endowed museum in the world.

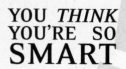

YOU *THINK* YOU'RE SO SMART!

What movie cowboy was never afraid to enter a bar and request his regular drink—milk—straight up?

TAKE A GUESS

You're a politician running for office. You do not have unlimited time or funds. So what age group should you spend most of your time and money courting, based on recent voting turnout percentages?

- O 65 to 74-year-olds
- O 55 to 64-year-olds
- O 18 to 25-year-olds

SO SMART: Hopalong Cassidy was the clean-living, honest-talking cowboy who loved his vitamin D. **GUESS:** Go for the oldest voting groups. Here's the breakdown: 55–64: 71% turnout; 65–74: 69%; 18–25: 34%.

TRUE OR FALSE

In Africa, you can hear African wild dogs barking.

FOR THE PARTICULARLY BRAINY

You're unpacking your suitcase in your hotel room. Alas, what did you forget?

MATCHUPS

On average, how many times have the following items been touched before being purchased?

1. Lipstick   A. 25 times

2. Towel   B. 8 times

3. Greeting card   C. 7 times

T OR F: False. Wild dogs seldom, if ever bark—that would scare prey away. Only domesticated dogs exhibit this sort of behavior. **BRAINY:** The top 4 most forgotten items are: toothbrush, underwear, film, and sunscreen. **MATCHUPS: 1** B **2** C **3** A.

NOW FOR THE REST OF THE QUESTIONS

1. In the Bible, what are the names of Adam's daughters?

2. You are enrolled in a class, learning all sorts of new stuff. How much of that "new" stuff is immediately forgotten?

3. After a day, how much new stuff you thought you learned is forgotten?

4. After a month, how much more of that information is forgotten?

5. What year did the office cubicle debut?

6. What militant atheist was shocked when her son revealed in the 1980s that he was a born-again Christian?

7. What percentage of burglaries takes place in the day?

REST OF THE QUESTIONS: **1** They are not named. **2** Memory experts claim that you forget more than 50% of the new stuff within a few hours. That's why you need to take good notes. **3** Yikes! 70% of new information is forgotten or purposefully discarded after a day. **4** Add another 10% for a total of 80%. It's a wonder how we can find our way home at night. **5** 1968. Up until then, most offices just held rows of desks. **6** Madalyn Murray O'Hair. **7** 60% or 6 in 10 are committed in broad daylight.

This Week in History: March 11, 1818.

Frankenstein by 21-year-old British author Mary Shelley is published. The book, in which a scientist creates a living creature from dismembered human body parts, is often called the world's first science fiction novel.

37

YOU *THINK* YOU'RE SO SMART

In order to be called an official drought, how long does it have to go without rain?

TAKE A GUESS

38

Milton Berle was a funny guy. Legend has it that he kept a few jokes on his computer. How many?

- O 1 thousand
- O 1 million
- O 6.5 million

TRUE OR FALSE

Gregor Mendel, the Augustinian monk whose work with pea plants established the foundation for modern genetics, was a child prodigy in biology.

FOR THE PARTICULARLY BRAINY

In 1896, a new ride debuted at Coney Island amusement park, drawing over 75,000 visitors. What was this cool new ride?

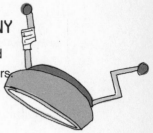

MATCHUPS

What are the 3 best-selling cookies in America from first to last?

___ Girl Scout Thin Mints

___ Chips Ahoy

___ Oreos

NOW FOR THE REST OF THE QUESTIONS

1. What's the most widely sung song in the English-speaking world?

2. How many American presidents have claimed to see a UFO?

3. How many times did basketball superstar Michael Jordan try out for his high school team?

4. What is the only state with a single school district?

5. What U.S. state has the most billboards?

6. If you are an average American, and we're sure that you are, and we give you a free 1-pound bag of M&M's, how many will you eat in a single sitting?

7. If we give you a free 5-pound bag of M&M's, how many will you eat in a single sitting?

40

REST OF THE QUESTIONS: 1 "Happy Birthday." **2** So far, just Jimmy Carter and Ronald Reagan. **3** Twice. He was cut the first time in his sophomore year. **4** Hawaii. **5** Florida. Anyone who has driven south through Florida can barely see the scenery because of the plethora of signs—the majority of which are luring you to the Ron Jon Surf Shop. **6** You will consume 112 of the delectable little bits of candy-coated chocolate, before you make someone take the bag away from you. **7** Without even thinking, you will eat 156. Candy experts say that the bigger bag provides an overwhelming sense of abundance, allowing you to eat more without worrying about running out or having someone else exclaim that you "ate the whole bag."

This Week in History: March 17, 1756. Glasses of Guinness are raised on this first celebration of St. Patrick's Day in New York City at the Crown and Thistle Tavern. It will take another six years (1762) for the St. Paddy's Day parade plans in NYC to come together.

YOU *THINK* YOU'RE SO SMART**!**

What is the only food that doesn't spoil?

TAKE A GUESS

Was tug-of-war ever an Olympic sport?

42

TRUE OR FALSE

The average cat will go back to its food bowl 37 times during the day to check on its contents.

FOR THE PARTICULARLY BRAINY

You're playing poker and are holding 2 black aces and 2 black 8s. You flinch, knowing you're in big trouble. What's the big deal?

MATCHUPS

Match the frequency to the percentage of how often adult siblings talk to each other:

1. Every few days   A. 7%

2. At least once a month   B. 20%

3. A few times a year   C. 44%

4. Never   D. 29%

NOW FOR THE REST OF THE QUESTIONS

1. What person in the Bible ate a scroll, found it sweet as honey, but later suffered some indigestion?

2. What do the following colors represent: white, purple, black, green, red, orange?

3. Who was the only U.S. president to be a prisoner of war?

4. Who was the only U.S. president never elected president or vice president?

5. Who was the only apostle from the Bible we know for sure was married?

6. Admiral Robert FitzRoy coined the term "weather forecasts" in 1861. Before then, what was the practice called?

7. What percentage of all car accidents is caused by sleep deprivation?

44

REST OF THE QUESTIONS: 1 John (Revelation 10:9-10). **2** The progression of colors of the carrot. It wasn't until the 17th century that carrots become orange, all through selective cross-pollination. **3** Andrew Jackson. The British imprisoned him in 1781 when he was 14 years old. **4** Gerald Ford. He was appointed vice president after Spiro Agnew resigned and was made president after Richard Nixon resigned. **5** Peter (Mark 1:30). **6** Weather indications or weather probabilities. **7** Over 50%.

This Week in History: March 21, 1980. U.S. President Jimmy Carter announces the United States' boycott of the Moscow Olympics, in response to the 1979 invasion of Afghanistan by the Soviets.

YOU *THINK* YOU'RE SO SMART

There are cold water oceans, or parts of oceans, and warm water oceans. If you want to find abundant ocean life, such as fish and plankton and all that, which ocean would you pick: cold or warm?

TAKE A GUESS

You're playing golf, having a good round and suddenly, without warning, an earthquake hits and knocks your ball off the tee. Does that count as a stroke?

SO SMART: Marine life is much more abundant in cold water than warm. Cold water can hold more dissolved gases—like oxygen and carbon dioxide—essential for fish and plants. More gas equals more living creatures. **GUESS:** Yep. Once you tee it up, if it falls off the tee, due to an earthquake or hurricane, or *anything*, it counts as a stroke.

TRUE OR FALSE

Elvis traveled a lot. He performed as much outside the United States as he did stateside.

FOR THE PARTICULARLY BRAINY

If you have a gun, hold it level and fire it, while simultaneously dropping a bullet from another gun barrel, which hits the ground first—the fired bullet or the dropped bullet? (Actually, you'd be a dexterous marvel if you could do both at the same time.)

MATCHUPS

Match the 1950 item with its price tag:

1. Gallon of gas	A. 62¢
2. Quart of mayonnaise	B. 20¢
3. Average income	C. $1,876
4. A pound of sirloin steak	D. $4.85
5. Average 4-door Ford	E. $3,216
6. Philco TV	F. $199
7. Long-playing (LP) record	G. 77¢

47

T OR F: False. Even though he was an international star, Elvis only performed outside the United States 3 times in his life. In 1957, he performed in Vancouver, Toronto, and Ottawa. That trip to Canada was it. **BRAINY:** They both hit the ground at exactly the same time. Gravity doesn't differentiate. **MATCHUPS: 1** B **2** A **3** E **4** G **5** C **6** F **7** D.

NOW FOR THE REST OF THE QUESTIONS

1. "Does she or doesn't she?" On average, how many American women dyed their hair in 1950?

2. Today is different. How many women dye their hair today?

3. What's the longest-running radio program in history?

4. In what year did the first hotel offer free soap in every room?

5. If you won a big boat, what would you pay to sail it through the Panama Canal?

6. Which is safer: taking off or landing in an airplane?

7. Who, in the Bible, fathered 70 sons by his many wives?

This Week in History: April 1, 1970.

President Richard Nixon signs legislation

banning cigarette ads on U.S. TV and radio.

49

YOU *THINK* YOU'RE SO SMART **!**

Is it *insure* or *ensure*?

TAKE A GUESS

50

How many meals have been "interrupted" by a mob hit? (My advice: Sit with your back to the wall.)

- ○ 3
- ○ 4
- ○ 5
- ○ 10

SO SMART: *Insure* and *ensure* can be used interchangeably to mean to "make certain." But if you're the Geico spokesgecko describing your services, only the word *insure* will pop up in your sales pitch. **GUESS:** We cross-referenced and found 5 people being forcibly exited from their earthly toil some time between the salad and dessert.

TRUE OR FALSE

In the Bible, King Abimelech had his armor bearer kill him so he would avoid the disgrace of being killed by a woman.

FOR THE PARTICULARLY BRAINY

Name the top 3 most intelligent dog breeds, and the 3 dumbest breeds, according to dog experts.

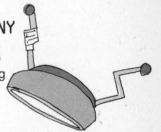

MATCHUPS

Match the celebrity to his or her shoe size:

1. Shaquille O'Neal	A. 22AAAA
2. Will Perdue	B. 22G
3. Michael Jordan	C. 13
4. Marilyn Monroe	D. 11
5. Paris Hilton	E. 7AA
6. Abraham Lincoln	F. 13

NOW FOR THE REST OF THE QUESTIONS

1. What story has been made into a movie the most times?

2. The director of the U.S. Patent Office said in 1899, "Everything that can be invented has been invented." Despite his statement, how many patents were issued in 2003?

3. If you really like kids, what state should you move to?

4. How many trips to the ER each year are due to playing the dangerous sport of Ping-Pong?

5. If you thought Ping-Pong was dangerous, how about shuffleboard? How many people are hurt each year playing this fast-moving game?

6. What was the first flavored chewing gum on the market?

7. If you want to increase your chances of avoiding a heart attack, what day should you sleep through?

52

REST OF THE QUESTIONS : 1 There are at least 90 film versions of *Cinderella*, using both actors and animation. The first film treatment was done in 1898. **2** 175,000. **3** Utah, which boasts the highest number of children per capita. **4** Over 1,500 people are injured yearly, usually by running into the sharp corner of the table while diving for a truly spectacular return shot. **5** Around 10 a year, mostly from getting hit in the head with a wickedly errant shuffle or hit on the head with an errant shuffle stick. **6** Black Jack (which was also the first "stick" gum) hit the local emporiums in 1884. **7** Monday. A 3rd of all heart attacks occur on Monday.

This Week in History: April 7, 1959.

Scientists at Los Alamos, New Mexico,

generate electricity from an atomic reactor

for the first time.

YOU *THINK* YOU'RE SO SMART!

What do more than 90% of all flowers have in common?

TAKE A GUESS

You've all heard the stories about the number of rats in New York City. What do rat experts claim the proportion of rats is to the city's 8 million residents?

○ 1 rat for every 100 people

○ 1 rat for every 10 people

○ 1 rat for every person

54

SO SMART: They either have no odor or an unpleasant one. **GUESS:** The experts claim that for every New Yorker, 1 rat slinks behind them.

TRUE OR FALSE

Ship captains can marry people at sea.

FOR THE PARTICULARLY BRAINY

How many U.S. presidents *never* made it to college?

MATCHUPS

Match the U.S. presidents with their secret service code name:

1. Richard Nixon   A. Eagle

2. Jimmy Carter   B. Trailblazer

3. Ronald Reagan   C. Searchlight

4. Bill Clinton   D. Deacon

5. George W. Bush   E. Rawhide

T OR F: False. The only way they *might* be able to marry someone is if they were also a justice of the peace or an ordained minister. Otherwise, most seafaring regulations expressly forbid a ship's captain from marrying people. **BRAINY:** 9. George Washington, Andrew Jackson, Martin Van Buren, Zachary Taylor, Millard Fillmore, Abraham Lincoln, Andrew Johnson, Grover Cleveland, and Harry Truman never earned a college sheepskin. **MATCHUPS: 1** C **2** D **3** E **4** A **5** B.

NOW FOR THE REST OF THE QUESTIONS

1. How many bugs do you think might be alive at any given moment?

2. This U.S. president was great friends with the prolific, blind hymn writer Fanny Crosby, famous for her songs "Blessed Assurance" and "To God Be the Glory," among almost 8,000 others.

3. When were the words "Once upon a time" first used in a book?

4. What was the only professional sport banned in the United States during World War II?

5. What is an "X-Y position indicator for a display"?

6. If you're going to sell a stock, what's the best month to do it?

7. What is the average height of a woman in the United States?

This Week in History. April 11, 1970. The Beatles' "Let It Be" hits No. 1 on the pop charts, 1 day after Paul McCartney formally announced the group's breakup.

YOU *THINK* YOU'RE SO SMART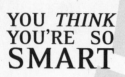

You have a degree in liberal arts. Just what are those liberal arts?

TAKE A GUESS

58

If you are the average world citizen, how much television do you watch every day?

- O 2 hours
- O 2.5 hours
- O 3 hours
- O 3.5 hours

TRUE OR FALSE

Hens sit on their eggs.

FOR THE PARTICULARLY BRAINY

How much fuel was left in the lunar lander when the first U.S. astronaut landed on the moon?

MATCHUPS

Match the most popular girl's name with its decade:

1. Emily   A. 1990

2. Jessica   B. 1970

3. Jennifer   C. 2000 (so far)

4. Mary   D. 1950

5. Linda   E. 1960

59

T OR F: False. They squat over them, supporting nearly all of their weight with their feet. So they don't really "sit" on their eggs, but hover just above them. **BRAINY:** 15 seconds' worth. **MATCHUPS: 1** C **2** A **3** B (Jennifer was first in the '80s too.) **4** E (There are a lot of Marys out there. She was the winner the in the 1920s, '30s, and '40s also.) **5** D.

NOW FOR THE REST OF THE QUESTIONS

1. How much did the IRS pay out as rewards to people who turned in a tax cheater in 2005?

2. Who is the only king in the Bible who is said to have no mother or father?

3. Do fish drink water?

4. How many little ridges are on the edge of a dime?

5. Name 3 star baseball players who, for a time, endorsed cigarettes.

6. It's a good thing he could remember his dreams. In the Bible story of Christ's birth, Joseph, Mary's husband, was warned in dreams to do 3 things. What were they?

7. What are your odds of being struck by a meteorite?

60

This Week in History: April 16, 1950.

The not-nearly-celebrated-enough author of this book, Jim Kraus, is born in relatively modest surroundings in Butler, Pennsylvania. He continues to stay relatively modest his entire life.

YOU *THINK* YOU'RE SO SMART!

What is the size of a meal at a restaurant compared to the same meal prepared at home?

TAKE A GUESS

62

If you are the average American baby, how much sleep do you need?

○ 13 hours

○ 16 hours

○ 18 hours

TRUE OR FALSE

There is an earthquake every day in Los Angeles.

FOR THE PARTICULARLY BRAINY

What was the first Hollywood movie to show a toilet flushing?

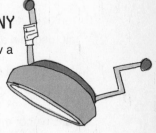

MATCHUPS

What are Americans afraid of? Match the fear with the percentage:

1. Speaking before a group
2. Heights
3. Bugs and creepy crawlies
4. Financial problems
5. Deep water

A. 22%
B. 22%
C. 32%
D. 41%
E. 22%

T OR F: True. On average, there are 1.2 earthquakes recorded every single day. Most, of course, are all but undetectable except by seismographs. Yet each year, Los Angeles slides 1/4 inch closer to San Francisco. BRAINY: *Psycho*. And that scene generated many complaints—many more complaints than about the violence and brief nudity.

NOW FOR THE REST OF THE QUESTIONS

1. Can you name the only U.S. state with an official snack?

2. You consider yourself reasonably clean, yet how many microscopic animals live on a square inch of your skin?

3. What biblical patriarch became so blind that he couldn't tell his sons apart?

4. Yul Brynner made his role in *The King and I* famous. How many times did he perform that role onstage?

5. If you are a mailman, what U.S. state should make extra-reinforced pants a standard uniform choice?

6. Peter Holden holds a dubious eating record. What is it?

7. What is the highest U.S. tax rate on individuals?

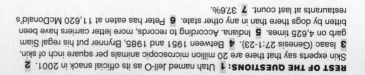

REST OF THE QUESTIONS: 1 Utah named Jell-O as its official snack in 2001. **2** Skin experts say that there are 20 million microscopic animals per square inch of skin. **3** Isaac (Genesis 27:1-23). **4** Between 1951 and 1985, Brynner put his regal *Siam* garb on 4,625 times. **5** Indiana. According to records, more letter carriers have been bitten by dogs there than in any other state. **6** Peter has eaten at 11,620 McDonald's restaurants at last count. **7** 37.6%.

This Week in History: April 27, 1995. The U.S. Air Force Space Command announces that the Global Positioning Satellite array is complete and fully operational.

YOU *THINK* YOU'RE SO SMART**!**

Name the only time a World Series was delayed by an earthquake.

TAKE A GUESS

Okay, let's say you're down on your luck, and you decide to start robbing banks. Morality aside, is that a good choice? What are the odds that you will get caught?

○ 50%

○ 75%

○ 90%

SO SMART: In 1989, an earthquake stopped a World Series game between the Oakland A's and the San Francisco Giants. The series was delayed a week, but Oakland eventually grabbed the trophy. **GUESS:** It's not such a good idea, since 75% of robbers get caught. That figure is misleading, too, since many robbers try their luck a second and third time, making the actual percentage of apprehension even higher. And the chance of pulling off a colossal heist is rare—the average haul is less than $2,500.

TRUE OR FALSE

Edmund Halley was very excited when he discovered the comet that bears his name.

FOR THE PARTICULARLY BRAINY

What is America's biggest piece of art?

MATCHUPS

What are the 5 top-selling board games in America, in order?

1. Scrabble   A. ____

2. Monopoly   B. ____

3. Trivial Pursuit   C. ____

4. The Game of Life   D. ____

5. Cranium   E. ____

T OR F: False. Halley did not discover it; he was the first to predict its regular appearance every 76 years. **BRAINY:** Mount Rushmore, of course. It was unveiled in 1941, cost $1 million, and attracts 2.7 million visitors a year. But truth be told, it was never really finished. World War II started and funds grew short, so the Mount Rushmore experts said the project was finished and sent everybody home. If you visit, make sure to look closely at Lincoln. He's missing an ear. **MATCHUPS: 1** Trivial Pursuit **2** Cranium **3** Monopoly **4** Scrabble **5** The Game of Life.

NOW FOR THE REST OF THE QUESTIONS

1. What are the top 3 categories of all advertising in America?

2. People have sliced bread since bread was first baked, but in what year did this non-baker invent the commercial bread slicer?

3. You make a phone call, are put on hold, and the music kicks it. If you really, really can't stand the music, where should you move?

4. Who was the first shepherd in the Bible?

5. Give me those old health-conscious movies. How many cigarettes did the lead characters in the movie classic *Casablanca* smoke on screen?

6. Who was the first U.S. president to have a telephone on his desk in the White House?

7. What is the average take-home pay for the American doctor?

REST OF THE QUESTIONS: 1 Automobiles, drugs (both prescription and over-the-counter), and movies. **2** In 1928, after 16 years of tinkering, Otto Rohwedder, a Missouri jeweler, built the first usable bread-slicing and wrapping machine. **3** Saudi Arabia. They have outlawed the practice. **4** Abel (Genesis 4:2). **5** They lit up 22 times. **6** Herbert Hoover. **7** The average doctor's salary is $189,000.

This Week in History: May 5, 1961.

Astronaut Alan B. Shepard becomes the

first man in space from the United States,

following a 15-minute, 28-second suborbital

flight in a space capsule launched from Cape

Canaveral, Florida.

YOU *THINK* YOU'RE SO SMART

In what country do 4 million golfers take out a special insurance policy to cover them if they happen to shoot a hole in one?

TAKE A GUESS

How many ways are there to make change for a dollar?

- ○ 212
- ○ 237
- ○ 248
- ○ 293

TRUE OR FALSE

Venus is the only planet in our solar system that rotates clockwise.

FOR THE PARTICULARLY BRAINY

If you are an average American, how much of the $100 that you spend annually on candy is spent on impulse candy purchases, like the Snickers bar at the counter in the gas station?

MATCHUPS

Match the inventor with his or her great idea:

1. John Deere   A. Snowmobile

2. Arthur Fry   B. Barbie doll

3. Walter Hunt   C. Windshield wipers

4. J. Armand Bombardier   D. Self-polishing cast steel plow

5. Mary Anderson   E. Post-it notes

6. Ruth Handler   F. Safety pin

71

NOW FOR THE REST OF THE QUESTIONS

1. Spam—how many Americans have eaten it?

2. Why should you never take a pig to the beach?

3. If you are the average American woman who has just gotten engaged, what are the odds that your prince charming gave you a diamond engagement ring?

4. How many minutes per week does the average American child watch television?

5. How many minutes per week does the average American child spend in meaningful conversation with his or her parents?

6. When did the first prize appear in a box of cereal? What cereal was it?

7. Who is the only person mentioned in the Bible as wearing graveclothes?

REST OF THE QUESTIONS: 1 Only 15% of us won't eat it. Hormel says 60 million Americans will. **2** Pigs can get sunburned in direct sunlight. **3** 8 in 10. **4** Nearly 1,700 minutes. **5** Only 40 minutes. **6** 1891. The prize was inside specially marked boxes of Quaker Oats. **7** Lazarus (John 11:44).

This Week in History: May 11, 1947.

B. F. Goodrich announces the development

of the tubeless tire in Akron, Ohio.

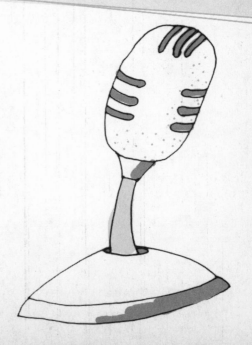

YOU *THINK* YOU'RE SO SMART

Why did Franz Liszt, the great 19th-century Hungarian pianist and composer, buy a long-haired dog even though he didn't like dogs?

TAKE A GUESS

74

Ah, football's televised instant replay. Too bad that referees can't see every one of them. When did it first begin?

O 1960

O 1963

O 1965

TRUE OR FALSE

John Wesley, founder of Methodism, was so busy writing hymns that he didn't preach very often.

FOR THE PARTICULARLY BRAINY

Of course you know him. Who was the brainy contestant with the longest streak of successful appearances on *Jeopardy!*

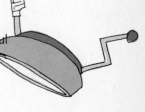

MATCHUPS

Match the event with the year that it happened:

1. Dale Earnhardt dies in Daytona 500 crash   A. 1994

2. Polio vaccine tested   B. 1975

3. Biosphere 2 opens in Arizona   C. 2001

4. *Exxon Valdez* runs aground   D. 1974

5. Honda Civic comes to U.S. market   E. 1989

6. Hank Aaron hits homer #715   F. 1955

NOW FOR THE REST OF THE QUESTIONS

1. If you like picture-perfect travel spots with no billboards to block your view, what 4 U.S. states should you head to?

2. When did the term *fast food* become part of the American vernacular?

3. How many prototypes did Thomas Edison make before perfecting the lightbulb?

4. How do clowns keep their faces straight?

5. When did someone last see the Ark of the Covenant?

6. What empire's taxation led to Jesus being born in Bethlehem?

7. What is the fastest fish in the world?

REST OF THE QUESTIONS: 1 There are no billboards in Alaska, Hawaii, Maine, and Vermont. **2** The term was first used widely in 1951 to describe "restaurants that specialize in serving meals within a few minutes of ordering." **3** 10,000. **4** In order to make sure no other clown duplicates their clown face design, clowns register their faces with a national clown face registry. **5** The ornate wooden chest that contained God's laws—the Ten Commandments—was taken to Jerusalem by King David. Eventually King Solomon put it in the Temple. It disappeared when the Temple was destroyed in 586 BC. And treasure hunters have been looking for it ever since. **6** Roman (Luke 2:1-7). **7** The wahoo, found off Florida and the Bahamas, as well as South Pacific waters. They have been clocked at speeds as fast as 60 miles per hour.

This Week in History: May 18, 1980.
A massive volcanic eruption of Mount
St. Helens in southwest Washington
devastates over 200 square miles of
wilderness. Fifty-seven people were
either killed or never found.

YOU *THINK* YOU'RE SO SMART!

When I was younger and more impressionable than I am now, someone told me that if you tossed a penny off the Empire State Building, by the time it hit the ground it would be going as fast as a bullet and kill whoever was unlucky enough to be in its path. Was I right to believe my brother?

TAKE A GUESS

How much money did Elvis make in 2004, nearly 30 years after his death?

78

SO SMART: No. Under the optimum conditions, with no wind at all, a penny might hit 100 miles an hour when it hit the ground. The slowest bullet travels faster than 600 miles an hour. And there are always updrafts around buildings. Those updrafts push against whatever is falling. Worst-case scenario: If someone gets hit by your tossed penny, it might sting like a bee bite, but the falling penny will not be deadly. However, our attorneys advise us to warn you not to go out and try it. **GUESS:** The money paid for royalties on his music and movies, plus fees for the use of his likeness in advertising, amounted to a paycheck of over $40 million.

TRUE OR FALSE

Lotteries are the scourge of modern culture and would have never been tolerated by America's founding fathers.

FOR THE PARTICULARLY BRAINY

Why does water come out of 2 holes in a drinking fountain?

MATCHUPS

Match the celebrity with his or her real given name:

1. Hulk Hogan   A. Paul Hewson

2. Peter Lorre   B. Allen Konigsberg

3. Patti Page   C. Clara Ann Fowler

4. Woody Allen   D. Ladislav Löwenstein

5. Bono   E. Terry Bollea

6. Sandra Dee   F. Alexandra Zuck

T OR F: False. George Washington ran a lottery to help pay for roads in rural Virginia. At the same time, Thomas Jefferson was petitioning the state of Virginia to allow him to hold a lottery to help him pay off his debts. **BRAINY:** Because 1 hole shoots out hydrogen and the other hole shoots out oxygen and when they hit each other, they combine to form water. Wait. We're pulling your leg. Fountain experts say the 2 holes produce a better, more rounded arc of water that is easier to drink. And the aeration makes the water taste better. **MATCHUPS: 1** E **2** D **3** C **4** B **5** A **6** F

NOW FOR THE REST OF THE QUESTIONS

1. In 1930, how long did the average pooch live?

2. How long does the average pooch live today?

3. What are the odds that you know how to play the piano?

4. Whose birthday in the Bible was celebrated with a lavish party fit for royalty?

5. New York City housing is pricey. What did a renter shell out for the average New York apartment in 2005?

6. Who was the first man to sail around the world?

7. A concern of all budding artists is the gray stuff inside the Etch A Sketch. That magic dust has to be poisonous, right?

REST OF THE QUESTIONS: 1 7 years. **2** 12 years. **3** 1 in every 10 people has taken piano lessons sometime in his or her life and can play the instrument reasonably well, making it the most played instrument—more than all other instruments combined. **4** Pharaoh's, while Joseph was living in Egypt (Genesis 40:20). **5** A little over $1 million. **6** Sir Francis Drake in 1580. His predecessor, Ferdinand Magellan, started such a voyage but died before the last of his ships made it back home. **7** Messy perhaps, but it is hardly deadly. The material is ground aluminum, pulverized so fine that it sticks to anything that it comes in contact with, like the Etch A Sketch's glass screen.

This Week in History: May 22, 1966. Bill Cosby wins the Emmy for best actor for his TV series *I Spy*. He is the first African-American actor to star in a regular dramatic television series.

YOU *THINK* YOU'RE SO SMART

Americans are a thoughtful people when it comes to presidential elections. They would never elect a president on the basis of how tall he was. Since 1888, how many of the shorter presidential candidates got the winning vote over their taller opponents?

TAKE A GUESS

82

As you get older, your body shrinks; at least most of you shrinks. Between the ages of 30 and 40, how much height does the average American lose?

- O 1/2 inch
- O 5/8 inch
- O 1 inch

TRUE OR FALSE

A monkey wrench is called that because it resembles a monkey's profile.

FOR THE PARTICULARLY BRAINY

Hawaii has a lot going for it, but it is the only U.S. state that doesn't have one of these. What is missing in Hawaii?

MATCHUPS

Match these schools with their unusual mascots:

1. University of California, Santa Cruz

A. Fighting Artichokes

2. Whittier College

B. Prospector Pete

3. Ohio Wesleyan University

C. The Poets

4. Scottsdale Community College

D. Battling Bishops

5. California State University, Long Beach

E. Black Flies

6. College of the Atlantic

F. Banana Slugs

NOW FOR THE REST OF THE QUESTIONS

1. True or false: Dragonflies are called dragonflies because they look like little dragons.

2. If you're traveling, you do *not* want to take your traveling Monopoly board to what countries?

3. If you are the average person reading this book, how many words a minute are you reading?

4. How fast was the fastest reader going before the literacy police made her stop?

5. How many Americans are not certain if anyone has ever dropped an atomic bomb in a war?

6. Which is correct—12 midnight a.m. or 12 midnight p.m.?

7. On August 1, 1981, what was the very first video aired on MTV?

REST OF THE QUESTIONS: 1 False. The name alludes to the fact that the insect has large eyes. Dragon is from *drakon*, which is a Greek word meaning "to look." **2** Monopoly is still banned in China, North Korea, and Cuba. It was once banned in Russia and East Germany. **3** 250 words a minute. **4** Anne Jones of England read nearly 2,300 words per minute. Later corrected for comprehension, her reading speed was reduced to a still astounding 1,285 words per minute. **5** Nearly 25% admit to not being totally sure. **6** Neither. Midnight does not belong to the day before or the day after—it is the dividing line between days. So the proper way to say it is *12 midnight, period.* **7** "Video Killed the Radio Star," by the Buggles.

This Week in History: June 2, 1979.

Pope John Paul II becomes the first pontiff

to visit a communist country when he is

welcomed by cheering throngs to his Polish

homeland.

YOU *THINK* YOU'RE SO SMART

Who was the only U.S. president known to have been treated by a psychiatrist?

TAKE A GUESS

You're stuck in the African bush. You come across an ostrich egg. You have a hankering for a hard-boiled egg. How long do you set the timer for?

- O 10 minutes
- O 20 minutes
- O 30 minutes
- O 40 minutes

TRUE OR FALSE

Charles Lindbergh flew the first nonstop transatlantic flight.

FOR THE PARTICULARLY BRAINY

Architecturally speaking, what are the 5 classical column types?

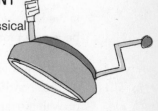

MATCHUPS

Match these women with the year and the "first" they achieved:

1. Elizabeth Blackwell
2. Elinor Smith
3. Mary Lou Retton
4. Geraldine Ferraro
5. Kathryn Johnston
6. Juanita Cruz

A. 1st female matador de toros (1940)

B. 1st American girl to play Little League baseball (1950)

C. 1st U.S. female doctor (1849)

D. 1st female to be featured on the front of a Wheaties box (1984)

E. 1st woman on the back of a Wheaties box (1934)

F. 1st female vice presidential candidate (1984)

87

T OR F: False. That honor went to John Alcock and Arthur Whitten Brown, who flew from Newfoundland to Ireland in 1919—taking over 16 hours to cover the distance. Lindbergh made the first solo flight—which is why he was called "The Lone Eagle."
BRAINY: I would have sworn that there were only 3 types, but actually there are 5. They are: Tuscan, Doric, Corinthian, Ionic, and Composite. **MATCHUPS: 1** C **2** E **3** D **4** F **5** B **6** A.

NOW FOR THE REST OF THE QUESTIONS

1. On average, how many American kids eat at McDonald's at least once a month?

2. In the Bible, what Old Testament person said he had become a brother to jackals and a companion to owls?

3. Horsepower is the ability to lift 33,000 pounds 1 foot in 1 minute or 550 pounds 1 foot in 1 second. Who came up with the term and the measurement?

4. On average, in a group of 100 Americans, how many of them have at least 1 sibling?

5. What was featured in the first TV infomercial ever aired?

6. How long do the majority of Americans hold on to a magazine?

7. How many times did Babe Ruth strike out?

REST OF THE QUESTIONS: 1 A whopping 90% of all American kids eat under the Golden Arches at least once a month. **2** Job (Job 30:29). **3** James Watt. He coined the term as he did additional work on the steam engine. And yes, he also named the measurement—a "watt"—after himself. **4** In a group of 100, 85 of them have at least 1 sibling. **5** The Chop-O-Matic infomercial aired in 1956. A spokesman for Chop-o-Matic is adamant that the phrase "It slices! It dices!" was *never once* uttered in the spot. Just in case you were concerned. **6** According to magazine experts, 50% of us hold on to magazines for 6 months. Another 20% of us hold on to them for years and years. **7** 1,330.

This Week in History: June 7, 1966.

Ronald Reagan makes the transition from

Hollywood stardom to politics by winning

the Republican nomination for governor

of California.

YOU *THINK* YOU'RE SO SMART

Why are carpenter's pencils square?

TAKE A GUESS

06

You're ready to leave the house for work, but wait! Your car keys are missing. Every day, on average, how much time do you spend looking for things that gremlins have snatched from you?

- ○ 4 minutes
- ○ 7 minutes
- ○ 10 minutes

SO SMART: So they don't roll off the desk. If we drop a pencil from our desk, it is no big deal. If a carpenter lets his pencil roll off the sheet of plywood he's using as a desk on the 90th floor of the high-rise construction site—that becomes a big deal. Square pencils stay put. **GUESS:** A frustrating 4 minutes a day—looking for keys, wallets, socks, small children—all the things that have mysteriously disappeared.

TRUE OR FALSE

The first coed dorm was "coedified" in 1956.

FOR THE PARTICULARLY BRAINY

You've heard the rumors. Are there alligators in the New York City sewer system?

MATCHUPS

Match the time spent in a store by a woman when she is with:

1. Another woman   A. 7 minutes

2. Her children   B. 8 minutes

3. A man   C. 4 minutes

91

T OR F: True. In 1956 the University of Indiana opened the first coed dorm, the men and women housed on separate floors. **BRAINY:** No. At least not now, according to the official version. Sewer workers did find a couple of alligators in the sewers in 1935, a 5-foot alligator in 1960 (probably flushed down the toilet when they were itty-bitty babies). But officials for the sewer system say they were all either shot or poisoned long ago. (Sure, sure.) **MATCHUPS: 1** B **2** A **3** C (hmm, why is that?).

NOW FOR THE REST OF THE QUESTIONS

1. How many of the nearly 500 criminals who have appeared on the FBI's Most Wanted list have been bad girls instead of bad boys?

2. Who was the first U.S. president to leave the country while in office?

3. In the Bible, what insect is held up as an example to the lazy man?

4. What percentage of Americans were involved in farming at the beginning of the 19th century?

5. Bill Gates has a little bit of money tucked away for a rainy day. How many countries have a gross national product lower that Bill's net worth?

6. Where in the world are Jews referred to as *Gentiles*?

7. How many people pay the $30 admission ticket to tour Graceland, Elvis Presley's home?

REST OF THE QUESTIONS: 1 Only 7 have been ladies. **2** Theodore Roosevelt, when he visited the Panama Canal Zone in 1906. **3** The industrious ant (Proverbs 6:6-8). **4** In 1810, more than 95% of the American population was involved in farming in some way. Today, only 2% of the U.S. population calls themselves farmers. **5** Compared to Bill, 132 countries make less money. Alone, Bill sits somewhere between the Ukraine and Morocco on the money scale. **6** Utah. All non-Mormons are called Gentiles by the Latter Day Saints. **7** Graceland draws 700,000 visitors each year.

This Week in History: June 16, 1884. Dads take their kids on a thrill ride when the first "roller coaster" premiers in the United States at Coney Island, Brooklyn, New York. It is called the "Gravity Pleasure Switchback Railway."

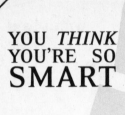

YOU *THINK* YOU'RE SO SMART!

Sumo wrestling has how many weight classes?

TAKE A GUESS

94

Has an X-rated movie ever won an Oscar for best picture?

SO SMART: None. The smaller wrestlers have to depend on timing, skill, and speed to best their much heavier opponents. **GUESS:** It sure has. *Midnight Cowboy* with John Voight and Dustin Hoffman was given an X rating when it was released. The movie won best picture in 1969. In 1971, the film was resubmitted to the motion pictures ratings board in anticipation of a rerelease. This time the board granted it an R rating. The rereleased version of the film was identical to the original.

TRUE OR FALSE

The phrase "In God We Trust" has been on U.S. currency since the beginning of our country.

FOR THE PARTICULARLY BRAINY

Why do we itch?

MATCHUPS

Match the generous country to the charitable donation made to the global poor:

1. Ireland

A. 7¢ a day per contributor

2. Norway

B. 5¢ a day per contributor

3. United States

C. 24¢ a day per contributor

4. Switzerland

D. 6¢ a day per contributor

T OR F: False. It was added to coins first during the Civil War–appearing on the 1864 2 cent coin; in 1957, the newly adopted national motto (adopted a year earlier), appeared on the $1 bill for the first time. **BRAINY: If** we have bug bites, fleas, a poison ivy rash or the like, it's obvious why we itch. But we're asking about that mysterious "spot" itching. Doctors really have *no idea* why that happens. But even if they don't know why, doctors came up with a name for it: *punctate pruritus*. **MATCHUPS: 1** D **2** C **3** B **4** A.

NOW FOR THE REST OF THE QUESTIONS

1. Who was Alfred Hitchcock's favorite actor?

2. How many prizes have been distributed in boxes of Cracker Jacks since their beginning in 1912?

3. What location marks the spot of the most deaths of American military men?

4. On average, what age group of Americans pops for the most plastic surgery procedures?

5. How many pieces of junk mail does the average American get each year?

6. What percentage of that junk mail is simply tossed away without being read?

7. You're facing your final days. Your dog is young and healthy though. Will you take care of your dog in your will?

REST OF THE QUESTIONS: 1 Why, Hitchcock himself. The portly film director had cameo or walk-on roles in 37 of his own films. **2** A mere 23 billion. **3** The state of Virginia, actually, because of the many Civil War battles fought there. **4** People in the 35 to 50-year-old age bracket get the majority of all procedures. **5** Just 575 pieces of unsolicited advertising every year. **6** Over 45% is discarded sans reading. Direct mail experts say they have less than 2 seconds to get a person curious enough to even open the envelope. **7** In the last will and testament of 27% of Americans, there is a mention or provision for their pooches.

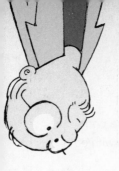

This Week in History: June 20, 1968. American sprinter Jim Hines becomes the first man to run 100 meters in less than 10 seconds, setting a world record at 9.95 seconds. His record isn't touched for 15 years.

97

YOU *THINK* YOU'RE SO SMART

Is there any bone in the body that does not connect with other bones?

TAKE A GUESS

98

If there are 100 boxer shorts out there, how many have been purchased by women?

- O 25%
- O 50%
- O 75%

TRUE OR FALSE

Napoleon was short and that's why he started so many wars.

FOR THE PARTICULARLY BRAINY

What's the difference between a hurricane and a typhoon?

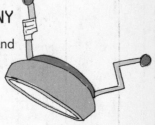

MATCHUPS

Match the inventor with his great idea:

1. Clarence Birdseye	A. electric motor
2. Edwin Perkins	B. miniature golf
3. Edward Lowe	C. frozen food
4. Garnet Carter	D. kitty litter
5. Michael Faraday	E. polio vaccine
6. Jonas Salk	F. Kool-Aid

66

T OR F: False. Napoleon was not short. He stood 5 feet, 6 inches tall, which was the average height for a man in the 18th century. The confusion about his height happened during his autopsy. French doctors listed his height in French measurements (*pieds de roi*) which subsequently did not get correctly converted to their English equivalents. **BRAINY:** Actually, nothing. They are the same thing except for the name. But traditionally, hurricanes occur in the Atlantic Ocean, while typhoons are found in the Pacific Ocean. **MATCHUPS:** 1 C 2 F 3 D 4 B 5 A 6 E.

NOW FOR THE REST OF THE QUESTIONS

1. Currently, how many blind people can read Braille?

2. What is the world's most popular last name?

3. How many times did Yankees' owner George Steinbrenner hire Billy Martin to be manager of the team?

4. Yes, it is true he couldn't hear anymore, but how long after Beethoven went deaf did he compose his Ninth Symphony?

5. In what year did the first amputee climb Everest?

6. What is the only insect that can move its head without turning its body?

7. How often is a bimonthly meeting held?

REST OF THE QUESTIONS: **1** Only about 10%. In the mid-1900s that number had been as high as 50%. **2** Chang. More than 75 million Chinese claim it. **3** 5 times, which coincidently is the same number of times that he fired Martin from that position. **4** 20 years. **5** 1998, Tom Whittaker climbed it after losing a foot in a car accident. **6** The praying mantis. **7** Bimonthly meetings are held every 2 months. Meetings held twice a month are sometimes called bimonthly, but the correct term is semimonthly.

This Week in History: June 27, 1929. Color

television technology is first demonstrated

in New York. (The next day, they air several

infomercials. Just kidding!)

YOU *THINK* YOU'RE SO SMART!

Pretend you're the dean of admissions at a fancy business school. You have a clearly unqualified candidate in front of you, but his parents pull out a check for $1 million and say that the school gets the money if their kid gets in. How much company are you keeping if you take the check?

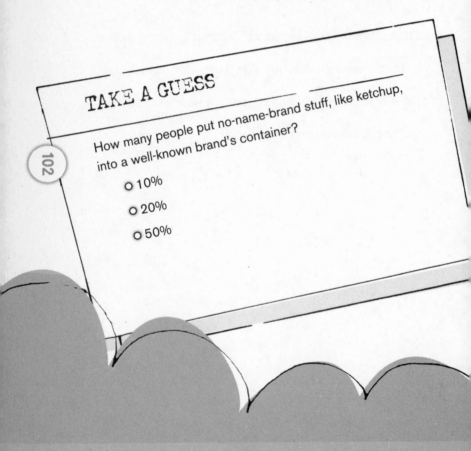

TAKE A GUESS

How many people put no-name-brand stuff, like ketchup, into a well-known brand's container?

- ○ 10%
- ○ 20%
- ○ 50%

TRUE OR FALSE

Sharks kill a lot of people every year.

FOR THE PARTICULARLY BRAINY

Why are the uniforms of professional Japanese baseball players printed with English letters and Arabic numbers?

MATCHUPS

Match the famous band/singer with their first band or given name:

1. The Beatles

A. The Warlocks

2. Chubby Checker

B. Arnold George Dorsey

3. The Grateful Dead

C. The Quarrymen

4. Doobie Brothers

D. The Blue Velvets

5. Engelbert Humperdinck

E. Ernest Evans

6. Creedence Clearwater Revival

F. Pud

T OR F: Pretty much false. In an average year, there are fewer than 100 reported shark attacks on humans. From those attacks there may be fewer than 25 to 30 fatalities worldwide. You stand a much greater risk of dying on the drive to the beach than you do from shark bites. **BRAINY:** You would think that they would use Japanese letters for their names. And the best reason we could find for why they don't—is because "it looks cool." **MATCHUPS:** 1 C 2 E 3 A 4 F 5 B 6 D.

NOW FOR THE REST OF THE QUESTIONS

1. Why is the phrase "You ain't heard nothing yet" remarkable?

2. Since the beginning of time, how many people have lived on our planet?

3. Who was the last king of Israel?

4. If you eat a cereal that claims it is "fortified with iron" does that mean that bits of metal will be floating around in your bowl?

5. The average American watches how much TV per day?

6. Name the Seven Virtues.

7. How many Americans have been killed by flying cows?

REST OF THE QUESTIONS: 1 Those 5 words were the first ones spoken on film—by Al Jolson in *The Jazz Singer*, the first talking movie released in 1927. 2 Depending on who you ask, the number is between 70 and 110 billion. 3 Hoshea (2 Kings 17:4). 4 Actually, yes. If you get a real powerful magnet, and run it through your cereal, you will attract small black bits of iron. Everyone needs a little bit of iron in their bodies, so no need for alarm. 5 An amazing 4.5 hours! 6 Faith, hope, love, prudence, justice, fortitude, and temperance. The Roman Catholic Church recognizes chastity, abstinence, liberality, diligence, patience, kindness, and humility. 7 At last count, 3. All have been involved in a car accident where a cow is hit and thrown, landing on top of them.

This Week in History: July 4, 1895.

"America the Beautiful" is first published

as a poem.

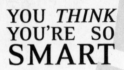

YOU *THINK* YOU'RE SO SMART

Who was the only person to actually sign the Declaration of Independence on July 4, 1776?

TAKE A GUESS

106

You have a great idea for a foolproof mousetrap. But you're not alone. How many different mousetraps have been patented over the years?

- ○ 1,000
- ○ 2,000
- ○ 3,000
- ○ over 4,000

SO SMART: John Hancock. The majority of the other signatures were added on August 2. **GUESS:** The total is around 4,400. *Every year*, nearly 400 people apply for a new patent on some variation of a mousetrap.

TRUE OR FALSE

If your house is on fire, you should be concerned about your diamond-encrusted tiara that you left in your jewelry box.

FOR THE PARTICULARLY BRAINY

When is it proper to use the word *irregardless*?

MATCHUPS

Match these baseball stars with the highest annual income they ever received while playing:

1. Babe Ruth		A. $100,000
2. Lou Gehrig		B. $42,500
3. Joe DiMaggio		C. $180,000
4. Jackie Robinson		D. $39,000
5. Ted Williams		E. $80,000
6. Willie Mays		F. $135,000

T OR F: True. You should worry, at least a little bit. Diamonds can burn. If heated to 1,400 degrees Fahrenheit, they will melt and convert to graphite. But that's the temperature of a blowtorch, not a house fire. But still . . . **BRAINY:** Never. The word is redundant because the negative prefix *ir* does the same work as the negative suffix *less*. Just say *regardless*. **MATCHUPS:** 1 E 2 D 3 A 4 B 5 F 6 C.

NOW FOR THE REST OF THE QUESTIONS

1. If you live in Schenectady, New York; Virginia Beach, Virginia; or Scottown, Ohio, your zip code is easy to remember. How come?

2. How long does your average American tabby live?

3. How much of that feline lifetime is spent sleeping?

4. When kitty is awake, how much time does she spend grooming?

5. Who committed the first murder in the Bible?

6. What U.S. president used to go skinny-dipping every morning in the Potomac River?

7. How many pairs of sunglasses have been turned into Disney World's lost-and-found department since 1970?

108

REST OF THE QUESTIONS: 1 In those 3 locations, the zip code numbers are consecutive. Schenectady is 12345; Virginia Beach is 23456; and Scottown is 45678. There is no 34567, in case you're wondering. **2** 15 cuddly (or not) years. **3** A normal house cat spends at least 65% of its life with its eyes closed. That doesn't mean kitty isn't thinking, though. **4** On average, a cat spends 12% of her life making sure every hair and whisker is spic and span and perfectly in place. **5** Cain, who murdered his brother Abel (Genesis 4:8). **6** John Quincy Adams. Imagine how hard it was to keep the local paparazzi at bay. **7** 1.6 million and counting.

This Week in History: July 11, 1981. In the United States, Neva Rockefeller becomes the first woman ordered to pay alimony to her former husband.

YOU *THINK* YOU'RE SO SMART

You are a tourist in New York City who spends the day in a couple of museums and shops before returning, exhausted, to your hotel. How many times were you videotaped by a surveillance camera today?

TAKE A GUESS

That mosquito that just bit you—was it male or female?

TRUE OR FALSE

Johannes Gutenberg made a name for himself printing playing cards before he started on Bibles.

FOR THE PARTICULARLY BRAINY

If you eat a hot pepper, what is the best way to cool the fire in your mouth?

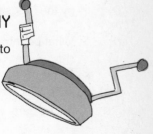

MATCHUPS

If something happens to the U.S. president, what is the line of succession?

1. Vice president
2. Secretary of the treasury
3. The president's wife
4. Secretary of defense
5. President pro tempore of the Senate
6. Secretary of state
7. Speaker of the House

A. 6th in line
B. 4th in line
C. Not in this line!
D. 2nd in line
E. 3rd in line
F. 5th in line
G. 1st in line

111

T OR F: That is true. Gutenberg printed playing cards before moving on to Bibles.

BRAINY: Most of the "hot" comes from the capsaicin in the peppers which stimulates the nerve endings. It does not dilute in water, so you are better off with a dollop of sour cream or yogurt, or a gulp of milk. **MATCHUPS: 1** G **2** D **3** C **4** A **5** E **6** B **7** D.

NOW FOR THE REST OF THE QUESTIONS

1. How long did the FBI investigate the song "Louie Louie" by the Kingsmen?

2. What country in the world has the highest literacy rate?

3. There were famous little guys and big guys in the Bible. Who was probably the most famous big guy and what did he carry with no effort at all?

4. How many women have appeared on U.S. circulating currency (as opposed to commemorative collectibles)?

5. How many barbershops were open for business in the United States in 1963?

6. How many barbershops are still going today?

7. What American university premiered the collegiate T-shirt?

REST OF THE QUESTIONS: 1 For 2 years. Somebody thought the lyrics contained offensive words, and using the best and most sophisticated electronic equipment available at the time, the FBI concluded that the lyrics were unintelligible at any speed. **2** Iceland, by far. Every citizen *must* graduate from high school. And to be eligible for a job, all candidates must speak at least 3 languages. **3** The giant Goliath who faced off with David, the shepherd boy, carried a spear that was as big as a weaver's beam (1 Samuel 17:7). **4** Aside from female representations of Justice and Liberty, only 4. Martha Washington was on the face of the 1886 and 1891 $1 silver certificates; Pocahontas was part of a larger engraving on the back of the 1875 $20 bill; Susan B. Anthony appears on the $1 coin first issued in 1979; and Sacagawea's portrait is on the Golden Dollar, a golden-colored $1 coin that came into circulation in 2000. **5** Over 100,000. **6** 44,000. **7** The University of Michigan started selling a T-shirt adorned with its name and logo in the 1920s.

This Week in History: July 22, 1955.

Disneyland, the $17 million theme park built

on 160 acres of former orange groves in

Anaheim, California, opens for business.

YOU *THINK* YOU'RE SO SMART!

According to video game experts, where do you find the donkey in Donkey Kong?

TAKE A GUESS

The most vertically challenged U.S. president was James Madison. How not tall was he?

- ○ 5 feet, 2 inches
- ○ 5 feet, 0 inches
- ○ 5 feet, 4 inches

114

SO SMART: You don't. Ever. There is a gorilla, of course, and Mario, and the fair damsel in distress, but not a single, solitary donkey in the whole game. There are various stories of why the name Donkey Kong was picked, but none of them have any reference to a character in the game itself. **GUESS:** President Madison stood proudly at 5 feet, 4 inches tall.

TRUE OR FALSE

We call the last finger the "pinkie" because it is the most pink.

FOR THE PARTICULARLY BRAINY

You're lost in the African jungle. All of a sudden, when you sniff the air, it smells like popcorn from the neighborhood megaplex. Should you be worried?

MATCHUPS

Match the most popular boy's name with its decade:

1. Jacob	A. 1980
2. Michael	B. 2000 (so far)
3. David	C. 1930
4. James	D. 1920
5. Robert	E. 1960
6. John	F. 1950

T OR F: False. It's not baby talk either—it is derived from the old Dutch word *pinkje*, which means "little finger." **BRAINY:** Jungle experts say that when tigers "mark" their territory, the smell is uncannily similar to the buttered popcorn smell in theaters. So yes, you should be worried, unless you can outrun a tiger, which you can't. **MATCHUPS:** **1** B The first 5 years at #1. **2** A (Michael takes the prize 3 decades in a row—the '70s, '80s, and '90s.) **3** E **4** F (Also in the '40s.) **5** C **6** D.

NOW FOR THE REST OF THE QUESTIONS

1. What percentage of Americans claim to have good relationships with their brothers or sisters?

2. How thick is the blubber layer on most whales?

3. Talk about sticker shock. What is the most expensive college in the United States?

4. What is the biggest church building in the world?

5. How big is the world's biggest church in terms of members?

6. What painting is the most popular art poster of all time?

7. Who was the world's first billionaire?

REST OF THE QUESTIONS: 1 Good news. An impressive 78% of Americans with siblings claim to have good relationships with them. **2** Generally, it is around 8 inches thick. A whale will not even bleed unless you can cut deeper than the blubber and hit the flesh beneath it. **3** Landmark College in Putney, Vermont, where tuition alone is over $35,000, without room and board. **4** Basilica of Our Lady of Peace, Ivory Coast, Africa. It was finished in 1990 and is modeled after St. Peter's in Rome. The basilica can hold 18,000 people. **5** Yoido Full Gospel Church in Seoul, Korea, has more than 800,000 members. **6** Vincent van Gogh's *Starry Night*. **7** John D. Rockefeller. At the beginning of the 20th century, his worth amounted to 1/44th of the U.S. gross national product, making him the richest American of all time.

This Week in History: July 28, 1977. The spigot is turned on for the 799-mile Alaskan Pipeline as it begins full operation.

YOU *THINK* YOU'RE SO SMART

You are dining out and have a hankering for seafood. The odds are that you will order a variation of America's most popular seafood. What is it?

TAKE A GUESS

What is the average length of a major-league baseball player's career?

- O 5 years
- O 10 years
- O 12 years

SO SMART: Shrimp. On average, Americans eat 3.4 pounds of shrimp in a year's time.

GUESS: There are some players who seem to never hang up their gloves, but the average career of a professional baseball player is 5 years.

TRUE OR FALSE

Mark Twain was the first American author to submit a manuscript created on a typewriter to a publisher.

FOR THE PARTICULARLY BRAINY

In what year of marriage do most divorces occur?

MATCHUPS

Match the number of billionaires to their country:

1. Japan	A. 3
2. United States	B. 55
3. Saudi Arabia	C. 15
4. Russia	D. 11
5. Germany	E. 33
6. South Africa	F. 371
7. China	G. 27

T OR F: True. In 1874 he bought a Remington typewriter and pecked out *The Adventures of Tom Sawyer.* **BRAINY:** Year 4 is the most risky. **MATCHUPS: 1** G **2** F **3** D **4** E **5** B **6** A **7** C (according to the *Forbes* February 2006 list).

NOW FOR THE REST
OF THE QUESTIONS

1. When did TV night owls get their first fix of late-night talk shows?

2. In the biblical story of the prodigal son, who was the irresponsible one—the younger or the older son?

3. It's the reason why the overhead bins for carry-ons in airplanes are so full. How many pieces of checked luggage are lost or misdirected every year by U.S. airlines?

4. Don't let your babies grow up to be hockey players. How many teeth did Gordie Howe lose in his first NHL game?

5. In 1993, how many U.S. patients had their stomachs stapled?

6. In 2004, how many stomach-reducing procedures were done in the United States?

7. Who was the first Ronald McDonald?

REST OF THE QUESTIONS: 1 In September 1954, *The Tonight Show with Steve Allen* hosting, premiered. **2** The younger son (Luke 15:11-32). **3** 30,000 pieces go missing. **4** 5 teeth. **5** 16,000 procedures were performed that year. **6** Over 125,000. **7** TV weatherman Willard Scott.

This Week in History: August 2, 1909.

The U.S. Army accepts delivery of the first

military airplane, built by the Wright

brothers.

YOU *THINK* YOU'RE SO SMART

One way you know New York City is an international hub is by the diverse nationalities of its cab drivers. How many New York cabbies are actually born in the United States?

TAKE A GUESS

How much of the water on the globe is salty, how much is fresh, and how much is frozen?

○ 97% salty, 1% fresh, 2% ice

○ 90% salty, 8% fresh, 2% ice

○ 95% salty, 4% fresh, 1% ice

SO SMART: In New York, 1 cab driver in 10 was born in the United States. **GUESS:** 97% salty, thanks to the oceans; 2% frozen in glaciers and ice caps; a mere 1% of the earth's water is fresh.

TRUE OR FALSE

A month that begins on a Sunday is a lucky month.

FOR THE PARTICULARLY BRAINY

When you park under a tree for a few hours in the summer, your windshield might get sticky. It's just a little bit of sap, right?

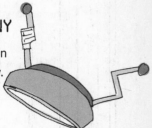

MATCHUPS

The diamond industry offers advice on how much to spend on your fiancée's engagement ring. Match the country to the amount:

123

1. Britain   A. 3 months' salary

2. United States   B. 1 month's salary

3. Japan   C. 2 months' salary

NOW FOR THE REST OF THE QUESTIONS

1. What are your odds of flying on an airplane with the same flight number as a plane that crashed?

2. After its first full year in operation, how many agents did the FBI have in the field?

3. How many agents does the FBI currently have working in the field?

4. This apostle of Jesus recorded his visions of the world's end times. Who is he?

5. To date, how fast was the fastest driver going before being slapped with a speeding ticket?

6. What U.S. state lays claim to the largest ranch?

7. Who makes more birthday wishes when they blow out the candles—men or women?

REST OF THE QUESTIONS: 1 0%. Flight numbers are always eliminated from rotation after a crash. **2** There were a grand total of 9 agents in 1909. **3** Nearly 12,000. **4** John. **5** In 2004, 20-year-old Sam Tilley on his motorcycle was clocked by a police helicopter at 205 miles per hour, 140 miles an hour over the speed limit. Do you think he used the excuse that he "was just keeping up with traffic"? Well, actually, Tilley claims he was neck-in-neck with another motorcyclist who got a ticket for a speed of 111 miles per hour. **6** Texas, of course. The largest ranch has more than 825,000 acres, roughly the size of Rhode Island. **7** Women, by far, at 75%. Only 20% of men make the same sort of wish. (I don't know about the other 5%—pets, maybe?)

This Week in History: August 12, 1992.
The United States, Mexico, and Canada agree
to form a free-trade zone (later known as
the North American Free Trade Agreement,
or NAFTA). It becomes the world's largest
single trading bloc.

YOU *THINK* YOU'RE SO SMART

How many words does the average American use on a regular basis?

TAKE A GUESS

Someone's given you his new phone number verbally, and you don't have a piece of paper to write it down. How long will the 7 numbers stay in your brain?

- ○ 15 seconds
- ○ 2 minutes
- ○ 1 hour
- ○ 3 days

126

SO SMART: It is doubtful if any individual uses more than 60,000 words, even though the English language has 600,000 words, plus 300,000 technical terms, the most of any language in the world. Word experts say the vast majority of our conversation and writing, some 90%, is handled through 1,000 words. **GUESS:** What? Who? Memory experts say that a new number, like a new phone number, will stay in your head for between 15 and 30 seconds, unless you make a concerted and repeated effort to remember it, thus forcing it into your long-term memory storage. Of course, you can also type it into your cell phone directory.

TRUE OR FALSE

The first talking doll was introduced in 1889.

FOR THE PARTICULARLY BRAINY

What put Vinko Bogataj on the worldwide map?

MATCHUPS

Match the event with the year that it happened:

1. *Titanic* sinks   A. 2000

2. 1st Internet Web browser   B. 2002

3. Elvis enlists   C. 1956

4. *American Idol* debuts   D. 1959

5. 1st moon landing   E. 1912

6. 1st VCR   F. 1958

7. Last original *Peanuts*   G. 1992

T OR F: This is surprisingly true. In 1889, Thomas Edison made 6,000 dolls with small phonographs built in. The doll was no Chatty Cathy in popularity, however: Edison only sold 1,000 of them. **BRAINY:** A spectacular crash. If you ever saw the opening segment of ABC's *Wide World of Sports*, Vinko is the unfortunate ski jumper who falls, flips, and crashes off the jump, going down in TV sports phraseology as the "agony of defeat." The 22-year-old Slovenian suffered a mild concussion but was back ski jumping the following year. **MATCHUPS: 1** E **2** G **3** F **4** B **5** D **6** C **7** A.

NOW FOR THE REST OF THE QUESTIONS

1. What year set the record for most movie tickets sold in the United States?

2. What is the largest private home in the United States?

3. You have problems singing America's national anthem, so be glad you're not from this country. What country is that?

4. What 4 creatures did God send as plagues on the Egyptians?

5. How many paintings did Vincent van Gogh sell during his lifetime?

6. How long does an eyelash last?

7. If you like coins jingling in your pocket, what country would you be out of luck in?

REST OF THE QUESTIONS: 1 More than 4 billion tickets were sold in 1946. **2** The 250-room Biltmore House in Asheville, North Carolina, built by George Vanderbilt. It was constructed between 1889 and 1895, covers 4 acres, and could fit about 88 average-sized homes into its space. **3** South Africa. The new anthem is an amalgamation of two previous anthems, changes keys in the middle (I'm musically illiterate but I am assuming that is bad), and is sung in *five* different languages: Xhosa, Zulu, Sesotho, Afrikaans, and English. **4** Frogs, gnats (lice), flies, and locusts (Exodus 8–10). **5** Only 1. He sold *The Red Vineyard* in 1890 for 400 francs. It is now on display in the Pushkin Museum in Moscow. **6** The life span of an individual eyelash is about 150 days. **7** Paraguay. It is the only country that does not use coins. Paper money is all you'll use there.

This Week in History: August 13, 1914.
Carl Wickman of Hibbing, Minnesota, creates
the first bus line in the United States and
names it Greyhound.

YOU *THINK* YOU'RE SO SMART !

If your toast falls from the kitchen table, what side lands face-down most often—buttered or unbuttered?

TAKE A GUESS

130

The late Supreme Court chief justice William Rehnquist had 4 gold braid stripes on the sleeves of his official Supreme Court robe. What did the stripes signify?

O chief justice status

O years of service on the Court

O military service

O nothing

SO SMART: If it falls from a kitchen table, it starts to flip and does not have a lot of room, so 2 out of 3 times, it lands buttered side down. If you are having breakfast on your roof, however, and the toast has some time in the air, 2 out of 3 it falls finds it landing on the unbuttered side, all this according to dropped-toast experts. (Actually, there was a university study on this.) **GUESS:** Absolutely nothing. Rehnquist's personalized fashion statement was inspired from a character's attire in a Gilbert and Sullivan operetta.

TRUE OR FALSE

A Shakespearean play was made into a science fiction film.

FOR THE PARTICULARLY BRAINY

Why don't we say "ahoy, hoy" when we answer the phone?

MATCHUPS

Match the country to the percentage of its churchgoers (at least once a month):

1. Ireland		A. 53%
2. United States		B. 67%
3. Italy		C. 60%
4. England		D. 12%
5. France		E. 19%

T OR F: That's true. *The Tempest* was the basis for the movie *The Forbidden Planet* in 1956. The producers took some liberties with the story, but they did credit Will for the idea. **BRAINY:** Alexander Graham Bell suggested that people answer the phones saying "Ahoy, hoy." But Thomas Edison liked "Hello" better. Up until that time, "Hello" was hardly used in common speech. According to phone experts, Edison's greeting won out because he was better at promotion and marketing than Bell. **MATCHUPS:** 1 B 2 C 3 A 4 E 5 D.

NOW FOR THE REST OF THE QUESTIONS

1. What is the only true American instrument?

2. Who was the female lead actress in *Lawrence of Arabia*, starring Peter O'Toole?

3. We know your child is really smart; after all, she was valedictorian of her high school class. So what are the odds of your offspring getting into Harvard?

4. What year were witch doctors banned from the African Cup games?

5. It's enough to drive a breadwinner crazy. What percentage of food, perfectly fine and edible, is purchased, brought home, and then thrown out before its time?

6. How many times are cats mentioned in the Bible?

7. Who was the only U.S. president who wasn't married?

REST OF THE QUESTIONS: 1 The banjo. It is native to the United States. **2** The movie lasted over 200 minutes and had a cast of thousands. But there was not a single speaking part for a woman. **3** Only so-so. In 2005, over 3,000 class valedictorians applied, and only 600 were accepted. **4** In 2002. **5** Americans toss out 14% of all purchased food while it is still totally edible. Most people keep an unwanted canned or bottled food item for over 2 years before tossing it out. Salad dressing is the #1 most discarded item. **6** They are never mentioned. I wonder if that is supposed to tell us something? **7** James Buchanan (1857-1861). Historians aren't certain why, but some presidential experts said it was because the 15th president suffered from a nervous twitch that caused his head to jerk frequently.

This Week in History: August 22, 1864.
Swiss humanitarian Jean-Henri Dunant
advocates for nonpartisan care of the
sick and wounded in times of war. The
International Red Cross begins its work.

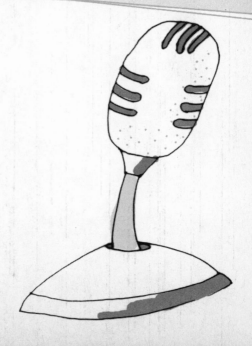

YOU *THINK* YOU'RE SO SMART

If structural engineers wanted to, could they straighten out the Leaning Tower of Pisa?

TAKE A GUESS

If your pet fish has a cold or a headache or is limping, how many veterinarians are there in the United States who treat fish patients?

- ○ 100
- ○ 500
- ○ 1,000

SO SMART: They really couldn't. Because the tower tilted in different directions during the first stages of construction, it has become curved like a banana and can never be truly upright and perpendicular. **GUESS:** No more than 100 vets make it a part of their practice to treat fish maladies. Some vets will also perform surgery on fish.

TRUE OR FALSE

Sweet potatoes and yams are the same thing.

FOR THE PARTICULARLY BRAINY

Name the seven deadly sins according to Thomas Aquinas's list.

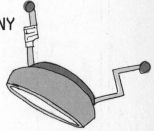

MATCHUPS

Match the inventor with his or her great idea:

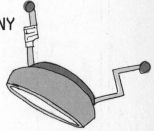

1. Charles Darrow — A. Liquid Paper

2. Samuel Morse — B. Outboard motor

3. Ole Evinrude — C. Erector set

4. Bette Nesmith Graham — D. Dr. Pepper soft drink

5. A. C. Gilbert — E. Monopoly

6. Charles Alderton — F. Morse code

135

1 OR F: False. Sweet potatoes are native to the Americas, first cultivated by the Aztecs, then picked up by the Spanish conquistadors. Yams are not grown in the United States—they have to be imported from the Caribbean or South America where they grow in tropical climes. Yams are starchy, but sweet potatoes are moist, sweet, and loaded with beta carotene. **BRAINY:** St. Thomas listed them as anger, covetousness, envy, gluttony, lust, pride, and sloth. **MATCHUPS: 1** E **2** F **3** B **4** A **5** C **6** D.

NOW FOR THE REST OF THE QUESTIONS

1. When did Walt Disney pull a fast one on us?

2. What are the two U.S. national monuments that can move?

3. How much do video game companies pay in rights to feature an animated version of a real NFL football player in a game?

4. What is the world's fattest tree?

5. How do you calculate the air temperature with a cricket?

6. What percentage of American men own a pair of khakis?

7. How many people actually heard Abraham Lincoln deliver the Gettysburg Address?

REST OF THE QUESTIONS: 1 In the 1958 movie *White Wilderness*, Disney movie-makers imported several thousand lemmings from Scandinavia, more or less forced them off of a cliff, and then claimed that the lemmings committed mass suicide. Amazingly, everyone seemed to accept this quirky story as truth. It isn't. According to lemming experts, lemmings do have surges in population every few years, and some may fall off cliffs looking for more open land, but there has never, *ever* been a scientifically documented case of mass lemming suicide. **2** San Francisco's cable cars and the St. Charles streetcar line in New Orleans. **3** To use actual names of ballplayers and their likenesses, the video people pay out over $250 million a year. **4** The pride of Tule, Mexico, is its cypress tree—measuring 164 feet in diameter. **5** Count the chirps in 15 seconds and add 40. That gives you the estimated temperature in Fahrenheit degrees. **6** Talk about a fashion staple—75% of American men own at least 1 pair. **7** A crowd of only 5,000 people attended the dedication of the battlefield cemetery on November 19, 1863, when Lincoln made his historic speech.

This Week in History: August 28, 1994.

Tiger Woods, 18, becomes the youngest winner

in history of the U.S. Amateur, a USGA

championship.

YOU *THINK* YOU'RE SO SMART

Take a poll of 100 average Americans and ask them about Elvis. How many still believe that Elvis is alive?

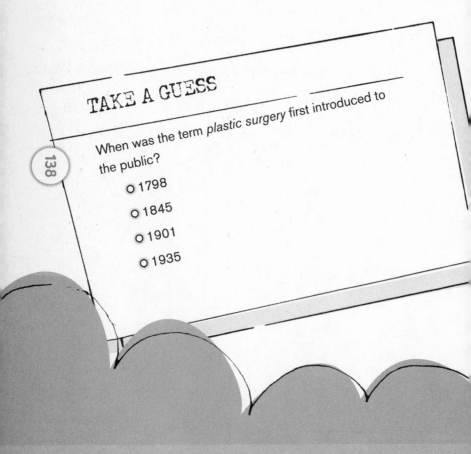

TAKE A GUESS

When was the term *plastic surgery* first introduced to the public?

- ○ 1798
- ○ 1845
- ○ 1901
- ○ 1935

138

SO SMART: 7 out of 100 will claim that Elvis faked his death to escape the pressures of being Elvis. **GUESS:** The term *plastic surgery* was first used in 1798 by a French physician.

TRUE OR FALSE

The first television rerun took place in 1956.

FOR THE PARTICULARLY BRAINY

Your plane has landed there—everyone who has ever flown has probably landed there at least once. So how did Chicago's O'Hare Airport get its name?

MATCHUPS

Match the pets to the presidents:

1. George Washington

2. Abraham Lincoln

3. Franklin D. Roosevelt

4. John Kennedy

5. Bill Clinton

6. Thomas Jefferson

A. Dick (mockingbird), Buzzy (dog)

B. Socks (cat), Buddy (dog)

C. Vulcan, Taster, Tipler (dogs)

D. Fido (first presidential dog to be photographed)

E. Fala, Tiny (dogs)

F. Charlie (dog), Macaroni (pony)

T OR F: False by a few years. In 1951, ABC reran episodes of *Dick Tracy*. **BRAINY:** The airport is named for Edward O'Hare, a WWII pilot who shot down 5 Japanese planes in the Pacific and is credited for helping save the U.S. aircraft carrier *Lexington*. He died in that battle. The airport code letters ORD printed on your luggage tags come from the place where O'Hare was built—formerly known as Orchard Park. **MATCHUPS:** 1C 2D 3E 4F 5B 6A.

NOW FOR THE REST OF THE QUESTIONS

1. What is the average salary of a college professor?

2. How many elevator rides do you need to take to get stuck once?

3. In 1900, how many eggs did the average American chicken lay in a year?

4. In 2004, how many eggs did the average American chicken produce annually?

5. When you are using crayons, which colors go to nubs first?

6. When was the first cell phone call made?

7. Is there a woman's name engraved on the Stanley Cup?

140

This Week in History: September 5, 1930. Two men from New York complete a 7,180-mile auto trip to Los Angeles and back in a 1929 Ford Model A—driven the whole way in reverse.

141

YOU *THINK* YOU'RE SO SMART !

If you are the average American, what is the maximum number of numbers your brain can store in its short-term memory file?

TAKE A GUESS

142

How many books did you and your fellow average Americans read last year, or at least the number you *said* that you read?

- O 8 books
- O 10 books
- O 16 books
- O 18 books

SO SMART: What? Who? Just kidding. The average number of numbers is 7: the exact number of digits in a phone number. Try to remember 8, and errors will dramatically increase. **GUESS: 16 books.** Of course, no one quizzed anyone afterward to make sure.

TRUE OR FALSE

Only 1 person in 3 thinks that "honesty is the best policy."

FOR THE PARTICULARLY BRAINY

Not every person in the medical world is health-conscious. As recently as 2002, what percentage of physicians in China smoked?

MATCHUPS

Match the celebrity with his or her given name:

1. Harry Houdini
2. Robert Taylor
3. Twiggy
4. Kirk Douglas
5. Chuck Norris
6. Judy Garland

A. Issur Danielovitch Demsky
B. Carlos Ray
C. Frances Ethel Gumm
D. Spangler Arlington Brugh
E. Ehrich Weiss
F. Lesley Hornby

143

NOW FOR THE REST OF THE QUESTIONS

1. What is the most malleable metal?

2. What does the *zip* in zip code stand for?

3. Does Bismarck, North Dakota, have anything to do with the Bismarck from Germany?

4. What is the shortest prayer in the Bible?

5. When did the last NFL player play without a face mask?

6. Here's a reason to stay in school. How many billionaires have been high school dropouts?

7. Have you ever seen a sleepy dolphin?

REST OF THE QUESTIONS: 1 Gold. A cubic inch of gold can be beaten into a leaf so thin that it could cover 1,400 square feet. **2** Zoning Improvement Plan. **3** Yep, it was a marketing strategy. Bismarck was originally called Camp Hancock, but was renamed Bismarck in 1873 in hopes of attracting German railroad investors. **4** "Save me, Lord!" shouted by Peter when he began to sink in the waves (Matthew 14:30). **5** Tommy McDonald, a Cleveland Browns' wide receiver played with a maskless helmet until 1968. But Pat Studstill, a flanker and punter for the Rams as late as 1971, always switched to a maskless helmet when he punted. **6** Only 18 that the billionaire trackers know of. **7** Dolphins do sleep—sort of. Their brains have 2 hemispheres just like humans, but the dolphin's brain lobes operate independently. For 8 hours the right side goes to sleep, for the next 8, the left side shuts down, and then voila! both sides wake up. During the sleep periods, the dolphin stays pretty inactive, but will wake quickly if danger shows up.

This Week in History. September 13, 1900.
While conducting experiments in Cuba to
determine how yellow fever is transmitted
to humans, doctor Jesse Lazear is bitten by
a mosquito carrying the disease. He dies
two weeks later, confirming the transmission
process.

YOU *THINK* YOU'RE SO SMART

Gather up 100 of your most average American workers and give them all a lottery ticket. If they all win 10 million dollars, how many say they won't quit their job?

TAKE A GUESS

How many shoes does the average American woman buy each year?

- O 2 pairs
- O 4 pairs
- O 6 pairs
- O more pairs than you can count

TRUE OR FALSE

A light-year is a measurement of time.

FOR THE PARTICULARLY BRAINY

If you are the average American person, how many times did you laugh today, including right now?

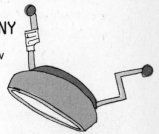

MATCHUPS

Match the superhero to his or her alter ego:

1. Spider-Man	A. Bruce Wayne
2. Batman	B. Bruce Banner
3. Supergirl	C. Diana Prince
4. Batgirl	D. Linda Lee Danvers
5. The Incredible Hulk	E. Peter Parker
6. Wonder Woman	F. Babs Gordon

T OR F: False, even if it does have a "year" in the terminology. A beam of light will travel 9,500,000,000,000 kilometers in a year. That *distance* is described as a light year. **BRAINY:** You're having a normal day if you chortle or guffaw about something at least 15 times. **MATCHUPS: 1** E **2** A **3** D **4** F **5** B **6** C.

NOW FOR THE REST OF THE QUESTIONS

1. If you are a politician and are running on a pro-Jell-O platform, where would you find the most receptive audience?

2. What country has the most frontiers?

3. If you are the average American man, how many hairs are there on your head?

4. What is the most popular street name in the United States?

5. Who were the first twins mentioned in the Bible?

6. What item (which we promise *would* fit down the pipes) is nearly impossible, if not entirely impossible, to flush down a toilet?

7. What animal never closes its eyes?

REST OF THE QUESTIONS: 1 Salt Lake City, Utah. They have the highest per capita consumption of Jell-O in America. **2** Russia has 14 different borders. **3** 100,000. **4** Park, because there are more Park streets, avenues, boulevards, places, etc. than any other street name. The rest of the popular names, in order, are: Washington, Maple, Oak, and Lincoln. Main Street is in 32nd place. **5** Esau and Jacob (Genesis 25:23-26). **6** A Ping-Pong ball. **7** A snake. It has no eyelids, only a hard lens over each eye. When it hibernates, its eyes remain open and staring. Scary.

WEEK 38
September 17–23

This Week in History: September 20, 1853.

American inventor Elisha Otis sells his first

elevator which he calls a "safety hoist".

True to its name, it was the first of its

kind to use a device to keep the car from

falling if the hoisting cable broke.

YOU *THINK* YOU'RE SO SMART!

What was the original game show on TV?

TAKE A GUESS

If you're in a hurry to have a baby, what animal should you be?

- ○ opossum
- ○ elephant
- ○ cat
- ○ dog

SO SMART: *Truth or Consequences* began broadcasting on a New York radio station first in 1940, then premiered on TV in 1950. Bob Barker came on board as host at the end of 1956. **GUESS:** Be the opossum. The American opossum bears its young 12 to 13 days after conception. On the other hand, the Asiatic elephant takes just over 20 months and cats (like dogs) have about a 2-month gestation period.

TRUE OR FALSE

An igloo is always made of ice and snow.

FOR THE PARTICULARLY BRAINY

What decision did Ron Wayne of Apple Computers live to regret?

MATCHUPS

Match the college/university with its sports nickname:

1. University of California, Irvine

2. Centenary College

3. South Dakota School of Mines

4. Columbia College (SC)

5. Columbia College (CA)

6. Our Lady of the Lake University

A. Claim Jumpers

B. Armadillos

C. Fighting Koalas

D. Gentlemen and Ladies

E. Hardrockers

F. Anteaters

T OR F: False. The word *igloo* is Inuit for "house". An igloo can be made of snow or animal furs or sod or driftwood. It really doesn't matter. **BRAINY:** In 1976, Ron sold his 10% stake in Apple Computers for $800 thinking it was going to cost him money to help keep the company afloat. That share would have been worth something in the neighborhood of $6 billion in 2004. **MATCHUPS: 1** F **2** D **3** E **4** C **5** A **6** B.

NOW FOR THE REST OF THE QUESTIONS

1. If you are the average American radio listener, how long do you listen during the week?

2. How many people will never touch a public phone?

3. To remain in orbit, how fast does the space shuttle have to go?

4. What do Kingsford charcoal and the Ford Motor Company have in common?

5. If you are the average American, how many of your fellow citizens have a tattoo?

6. How many average Americans regret ever having gotten their tattoos?

7. If you want to avoid having your house burglarized, what month should you stay home?

REST OF THE QUESTIONS: **1** This one surprised me. The average American spends 20 hours per week listening to the radio, or at least having it on while nearby. **2** 50% say they might not touch a public phone even in an emergency. **3** 17,500 miles an hour. **4** Henry Ford. In the 1920s, Ford was disturbed over how much wood his plants discarded. He convinced his cousin, Edward Kingsford, to recycle the wood scraps into charcoal briquettes. Henry was full of ideas. **5** 30 million have been inked. **6** Nearly 20%. **7** August. More home invasions take place in August compared with any other month.

This Week in History: September 25, 1956. The first transatlantic telephone call is placed between New York City and London, England, over the newly installed transatlantic telephone cable. The technological marvel could handle 36 calls simultaneously.

YOU *THINK* YOU'RE SO SMART!

You should be relieved when a jury finds you innocent.

TAKE A GUESS

How much did it cost, on average, for a wedding in 2004?

- ○ $17,500
- ○ $20,000
- ○ $23,000
- ○ $27,000

SO SMART: A jury *cannot* find you innocent. They can only find you guilty or not guilty. There is that "beyond a reasonable doubt" aspect to a jury's findings. **GUESS:** The average American wedding in 2004 cost the bride's parents close to $23,000.

TRUE OR FALSE

You digest your food in your stomach.

FOR THE PARTICULARLY BRAINY

Floyd Rood made history by golfing across America in 1963. How many shots did he take during the 13-month journey?

MATCHUPS

Match the country with the length of its school year:

1. China   A. 243 days

2. Japan   B. 180 days

3. Germany   C. 251 days

4. Italy   D. 196 days

5. England   E. 226 days

6. United States   F. 216 days

155

NOW FOR THE REST OF THE QUESTIONS

1. What makes us yawn?

2. What percentage of people yawn when they see someone else yawn?

3. What percentage of people yawn after they read about yawning?

4. In the Bible, who was the criminal in the Bible who the people in Jerusalem wanted Pilate to release instead of Jesus?

5. What is the only 8-letter English word with only 1 vowel?

6. If you are the average American, what are the odds you have used your cell phone in the bathroom?

7. Why was Voltaire such a prolific writer?

REST OF THE QUESTIONS: 1 All sorts of things, including boring people, but the physical reason is this: If we are sitting in a stuffy room, we tend to breathe more slowly and our body doesn't get all the oxygen it needs. Our brain senses this and sends a signal to the lungs to take an extra deep breath. That extra deep breath is called a yawn. **2** 50%. **3** 65%. **4** Barabbas (Luke 23:18). **5** Strength. **6** A clear majority—6 in 10 of us. Hey! It's private. **7** Allegedly, Mr. Voltaire consumed up to 70 cups of coffee a day.

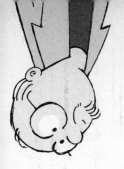

This Week in History: October 4, 1957. The Soviet Union launches *Sputnik*, the world's first artificial satellite which is 22 inches in diameter and weighs 183 pounds. A person with a good pair of binoculars could see it at night. Dismayed that the Soviets have beaten them into space, America's space program gets into hyperdrive.

157

YOU *THINK* YOU'RE SO SMART **!**

You're sitting in coach on an airplane enjoying your root beer while staring at the Rocky Mountains from 30,000 feet up. All of a sudden, you hear two loud chimes. What do they signify?

TAKE A GUESS

How wide is the average bolt of lightning?

- O 1 foot
- O 2 feet
- O 5 inches
- O 1/2 inch

SO SMART: It sort of depends on what airline you're on, and even what specific airplane. Each airline does have its own chime code to alert the crew in case of an emergency. Most of the time, those chimes are just someone in the cockpit calling various members of the crew, perhaps alerting them about upcoming air turbulence, or more likely, as a pilot admitted, to ask someone to bring fresh coffee. **GUESS:** You don't have to be wide to be deadly—lightning bolts average about 1/2 inch wide with a temperature 5 times as hot as the sun.

TRUE OR FALSE

A curveball curves.

FOR THE PARTICULARLY BRAINY

Would you rather be food-deprived or sleep-deprived for a month?

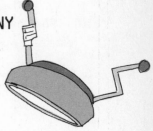

MATCHUPS

Match up the person with where his or her final ashes were buried or scattered:

159

1. Joy Adamson	A. Lake Michigan
2. Aaron Copeland	B. Atlantic Ocean
3. Maria Callas	C. Tanglewood
4. John F. Kennedy Jr.	D. Buried with a lioness
5. Ann Landers	E. Aegean Sea

NOW FOR THE REST OF THE QUESTIONS

1. Who was the only president to be blind in 1 eye?

2. In 1955, the standard tip in the standard American restaurant was 5%. What is it today?

3. A tip for the waitresses: If you draw a smiley face on the check, how much will that likely increase the percentage of your tip?

4. You pick up an item at the grocery store. Let's say it is a box of Frosted Flakes. Then two aisles later, you remember that you don't like Frosted Flakes. Do you take it back to the cereal aisle?

5. Of course, we all know that Mahatma Gandhi won the Nobel Peace Prize. What year did he win?

6. Who is the only person more recognizable to school children than Ronald McDonald?

7. What biblical epic, starring Charlton Heston, was the top movie moneymaker of the 1950s?

REST OF THE QUESTIONS: 1 Theodore Roosevelt. He was injured in a boxing match in 1904. By 1908 he was totally blind in his left eye, but the condition was kept secret. **2** 18.5%. **3** 18%—time to take drawing lessons! **4** Only 1 shopper in 3 will return the item to its original location. **5** This is a trick question. Gandhi was nominated in 1937, 1938, 1939, 1947, and 1948, but he never won. Nobel Prize experts said that he would have won in 1948, but he was assassinated only days before the ceremony. And the Nobel Peace Prize people never give the award posthumously. **6** Ho-ho-ho—it's Santa—with Ronald in 2nd place. **7** *The Ten Commandments* with Heston playing a memorable Moses.

This Week in History: October 12, 1960.

At the UN, Soviet leader Nikita Khrushchev

removes his shoe and pounds a table,

protesting against a speech critical of

Soviet policy in Eastern Europe.

YOU *THINK* YOU'RE SO SMART

If you make your bed every day, are you in the majority or minority?

TAKE A GUESS

When you jumped in your Conestoga wagon and headed to the great American West, how fast did you go after you commanded your horse to "giddyup"?

- O 1 mile an hour
- O 2 miles an hour
- O 3 miles an hour
- O 4 miles an hour

162

SO SMART: Majority. The bed-making slackers—those who occasionally make it—number about 21%. And another 5%—super slackers—claim *never* to make their bed.

GUESS: No one headed west very quickly. Wagon trains averaged about 2 miles an hour, which was good news for any toddler who fell off the wagon because that is the walking speed of a toddler.

TRUE or FALSE

Black widow spiders kill and eat their mates after they mate.

FOR THE PARTICULARLY BRAINY

Who was the more prolific philosophical writer, Socrates or Plato?

MATCHUPS

Match the original name to the current name for these products:

1. Reno inclined elevator   A. Popsicle

2. Waist overalls   B. Ballpoint pen

3. Nonleaking writing stick   C. Blue jeans

4. Epsicle   D. Alka-Seltzer

5. Aspirvess   E. Escalator

163

T OR F: We'll take both true and false as correct answers. *Most of the time,* the ladies do indeed dispatch their husbands quickly after the wedding ceremony. But not always. Spider experts are still unsure of what makes the average lady black widow homicidal. **BRAINY:** A trick question. Socrates never wrote anything down. All his teachings were recorded by his student, Plato. **MATCHUPS: 1** E **2** C **3** B **4** A **5** D.

NOW FOR THE REST
OF THE QUESTIONS

1. Paul Revere shouted "The British are coming" during his midnight ride in Boston. True or false?

2. Pablo Picasso enjoyed explaining his work to curious art lovers. True or false?

3. The only ingredient you can't add to Jell-O is pineapple.

4. In 1980, what was the percentage of American comedians who were Jewish?

5. In the Bible, how did God first appear to Moses?

6. What is the only nation where a map of the country is depicted on the national flag?

7. This famous mountain's name is just a letter and a number. Can you name it?

REST OF THE QUESTIONS: 1 False. He shouted, "The regulars are out." The regulars were the British infantry soldiers. Since there were many British people in the colonies, it would have made no sense to warn them about the British. **2** False. Picasso loathed it. In fact, he started carrying a revolver loaded with blanks so he could fire at any "peasant" who asked for an explanation of what those funny shapes were supposed to represent. **3** That is mostly false. We like destroying long-held illusions. Admittedly, *fresh* pineapple contains stuff called *bromelain*, which is like Jell-O kryptonite and prevents it from jelling. But if you use *canned* pineapple, the heat in the canning process destroys the bromelain and lets you complete that delicious molded Jell-O salad whenever you've got a taste for it. **4** 80% were Jewish. **5** In a burning bush that did not burn up, described in Exodus 3:2. **6** Cyprus. **7** The world's 2nd tallest mountain is called K2, because it is in the Karakoram segment of the Himalayas between Pakistan and China and is the 2nd highest in the world.

This Week in History: October 19, 1936. In a race around the world using only commercial airlines, H. R. Elkins, a *Scripps-Howard* reporter, beats his competitors, including crime reporter Dorothy Kilgallen. His round-the-world time: 18.5 days.

YOU *THINK* YOU'RE SO SMART

What is the rarest fish in the world?

TAKE A GUESS

166

In 2006, the average price for a ticket to a big-name tour concert was:

- ○ $56.88
- ○ $59.75
- ○ $61.45
- ○ $74.95

SO SMART: The oarfish, a long ribbonlike fish, is often confused with sea monsters if they wash up on shore. Because they are found in the deep ocean, they are rarely seen. They can range in size from 26 feet to almost 56 feet in length, according to some reports. **GUESS:** Concertgoers shelled out $61.45 on average, up from 2005's ticket price of $56.88. The top moneymaker? The Rolling Stones who grossed $138.5 million in ticket sales.

TRUE OR FALSE

You are safe from tornadoes if you live in a big city.

FOR THE PARTICULARLY BRAINY

Name the U.S. city in which all the professional sports teams wear the same colors.

MATCHUPS

Match the plastic surgery procedure to its average U.S. cost:

1. Face-lift	A. $6,000–$8,000
2. Hair removal	B. $200–$400
3. Nose surgery	C. $7,000–$9,000
4. Tummy tuck	D. $2,500–$4,500
5. Botox (per area)	E. $300–$800
6. Liposuction (per area)	F. $5,000–$6,000

T OR F: False. Tornadoes do not often enter into big cities, but they can and have. Tornadoes have hit the downtown areas of Salt Lake City, Miami, Nashville, and Fort Worth, just to name a few. It appears that if a tornado wants to head down Michigan Avenue in Chicago, no one will be able to tell it that it shouldn't be there. **BRAINY:** Pittsburgh. All the teams of the city wear uniforms of black and gold. **MATCHUPS: 1** C **2** E **3** F **4** A **5** B **6** D.

NOW FOR THE REST OF THE QUESTIONS

1. Has any U.S. president ever received a patent?

2. What's the difference between "partly cloudy" and "partly sunny"?

3. You're in a face-off with a skunk. He missed you with his first 5 shots of nasty-smelling spray. How many shots does he have left?

4. If you really like making movies, where should you live?

5. How many Web pages were on the Internet in 1995?

6. How many Web pages were up and running in 2004?

7. In 2001, some 10% of all American college students confessed to plagiarizing from an Internet source. How many admitted to the same infraction just 3 years later?

REST OF THE QUESTIONS: 1 Only 1—Abraham Lincoln. He devised some sort of device with bellows and pulleys to float boats over shallow water. The device never took off—but they do use the principle when floating submarines. **2** According to official government rules for weather forecasting, if 40–70% of the sky is expected to be cloudy, the forecast is "partly cloudy." If the clouds are less than 40%, then the forecast is "partly sunny." No clouds mean "clear," and more than 70% cloud cover is "cloudy." **3** You're not out of the woods yet (but I'd head there fast). The average skunk has 6 shots of scent which can be sprayed up to 10 feet. **4** Bombay, India. Over 1,000 movies are made there every year, twice what Hollywood makes. **5** 1.3 million. **6** 8 billion. **7** Over 40%.

This Week in History: October 24, 1939.

The first nylon stockings, intended by their manufacturer, DuPont, to replace costly silk stockings, go on sale in New York City.

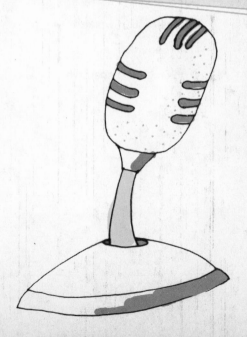

YOU *THINK* YOU'RE SO SMART

Are brains expanding or shrinking over time, like over centuries and centuries?

TAKE A GUESS

170

What is the most dangerous job in America?

- O fireman
- O policeman
- O construction worker
- O garbageman
- O commercial fisherman

SO SMART: Most scientists agree that our brains are 10 to 15% smaller than they were when we were living out in the wild. There are theories why this is happening, but no proof. **GUESS:** According to the National Safety Council, the most dangerous job is garbageman. They have more injuries per man-hour than any other profession. They may not have the same number of fatal accidents as the other professions, but they are hurt most often.

TRUE OR FALSE

Laughing at sitcoms can be subjective. But then TV producers solved the problem with the laugh track, introduced in 1950.

FOR THE PARTICULARLY BRAINY

The first jack-o'-lanterns were made from what vegetable?

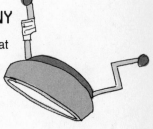

MATCHUPS

Match the famous person with 1 of his famous nicknames:

1. Buster Keaton   A. The Man of a
                             Thousand Faces

2. Arnold   B. The Greatest
   Schwarzenegger

3. Muhammad Ali   C. Spark Plug

4. Elijah Wood   D. The Austrian Oak

5. Lon Chaney Sr.   E. The Great Stone Face

NOW FOR THE REST OF THE QUESTIONS

1. The coffee break has been around for a long time, right?

2. What are the odds that you know someone, are someone, or are related to someone who is obsessed with germs?

3. In 1965, you could have bought 1 share of Berkshire Hathaway stock for $18. What was 1 share of the stock worth in 2004?

4. Arrange these five wild animals (considered the loudest of all animals) from loudest to least loud: wolf, sea lion, elephant, lion, and elk.

5. Do fish sweat?

6. If there *is* a ghost in the White House, who do most of the people who have seen it claim it is?

7. What two sin-filled cities were destroyed by fire and brimstone from heaven?

REST OF THE QUESTIONS: 1 Actually within the Baby Boomers' lifetime. The phrase was coined in an advertising campaign for coffee in the early 1950s. Within a few years, virtually every business had instituted some sort of coffee break time. **2** 1 in 5 Americans admit to being somewhat phobic about germs. **3** A little bit of foresight would have been nice—over $85,000! **4** The lion's roar takes the prize, followed by the elk, sea lion, wolf, and elephant. **5** No. Well, maybe—sort of. But they don't sweat water that cools them off like humans and animals. Saltwater fish do build up salt in their bodies and that extra salt is "sweated" out through special salt cells. Long answer short, no, they don't really sweat like humans. **6** Abe Lincoln. **7** Sodom and Gomorrah (Genesis 19:24).

172

This Week in History: October 31, 1517. Martin Luther, a professor of biblical interpretation at the University of Wittenberg, nails a paper with his 95 theses to the door of Castle Church. This marks the beginning of the Protestant Reformation in Germany.

YOU *THINK* YOU'RE SO SMART

Why don't birds that perch on high voltage wires get electrocuted?

TAKE A GUESS

174

It sure seems like there are more commercials on TV than actual shows. On average, how much of every hour is taken up with commercials?

O 9 minutes

O 13 minutes

O 16 minutes

O 20 minutes

SO SMART: Because they are not grounded, nor do they complete a circuit. However, if they touched the ground and the wire simultaneously, they'd fry. That would mean, of course, that they were one BIG bird. **GUESS:** The correct answers are 16 minutes and 20 minutes. On the big 3 networks, at least 16 minutes of every hour is advertising. On most cable channels, advertising takes up 20 minutes and sometimes more.

TRUE _{OR} FALSE

The *Mona Lisa* in the Louvre has always been super-protected, even back in the early part of the 1800s.

FOR THE PARTICULARLY BRAINY

Who was the youngest person to ever earn a million dollars through his or her own efforts?

MATCHUPS

Match the celebrity with his given name:

1. Boris Karloff
2. Curly Howard
3. The Rock
4. Fred Astaire
5. Ringo Starr
6. Jack Black

A. Dwayne Johnson
B. Thomas Black
C. William Henry Pratt
D. Jerome Lester Horwitz
E. Frederick Austerlitz
F. Richard Starkey

T OR F: False. At the end of the 19th century, there wasn't high security in museums. In 1911, a Louvre employee made off with the iconic painting hidden under his coat during the museum's regular hours. He was in cahoots with a forger. Two years later, when the thief tried to sell the original Da Vinci, he was caught and the painting returned—with maximum security in place. BRAINY: Shirley Temple. By the time she was 10, she had amassed over a million dollars. She began acting at age 3 in 1931. MATCHUPS: 1 C 2 D 3 A 4 E 5 F 6 B.

NOW FOR THE REST OF THE QUESTIONS

1. What was the busiest day ever for long-distance cell phone calls?

2. What do the following vegetables have in common: tomatoes, cucumbers, eggplants, peppers, string beans?

3. Chicago is really the windiest city in America, right?

4. We have all seen the big bug swarms in horror movies and old biblical epic movies. How large was the largest locust swarm ever recorded?

5. How many people in the United States just don't go to the dentist because they fear the possible pain?

6. What kind of wood was Noah's ark made of?

7. What is the only continent without mold or mildew?

REST OF THE QUESTIONS: 1 September 11, 2001. **2** None of them are vegetables, in the true, scientific sense. (Tell that to my 9-year-old). **3** Nope. Chicago's average wind speed is 10 miles an hour, good for only 16th on the list. The top 5 are: Great Falls, Montana at 13.1; Oklahoma City, Oklahoma at 13; Boston, Massachusetts at 12.9; Cheyenne, Wyoming, at 12.8; and Wichita, Kansas at 12.7. **4** In 1954, 1 swarm consisting of 10 billion locusts covered over 125 square miles of Kenya. **5** 15%. In Britain, the number jumps to nearly 40%. **6** You get points for either cypress or gopher wood (Genesis 6:14). **7** Antarctica.

This Week in History: November 6, 1928. The first electric flashing sign signals election results from all 4 sides of the New York Times Building in New York City. The sign used more than 14,000 bulbs and 1 million feet of copper wire.

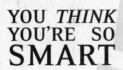

YOU *THINK* YOU'RE SO SMART!

Why don't ants drown in a heavy rain?

TAKE A GUESS

Give or take a few thousand, how many babies were born in the United States last year?

- O 3 million
- O 3.7 million
- O 4 million
- O 4.4 million

SO SMART: It's really, really hard to drown an ant. You can keep an ant in water for hours, or even days, and even if it looks drowned, it often isn't. Set it on dry land in the sun for a couple of hours and it will revive. The reason that water doesn't penetrate an ant's teeny, tiny breathing tubes is that there is too much surface tension. **GUESS:** Last year 4,093,000 babies were born in the United States, so 4 million is closest.

TRUE ᴏʀ FALSE

The majority of people in the United States can roll their tongues.

FOR THE PARTICULARLY BRAINY

According to advertising experts, what is the most enduring, most recognizable advertising icon of the 20th century?

MATCHUPS

Match the holiday to where it lines up in candy sales:

1. Easter   A. 1st

2. Christmas   B. 2nd

3. Halloween   C. 3rd

4. Valentine's Day D. 4th

179

NOW FOR THE REST OF THE QUESTIONS

1. Who held the top 5 positions on the music singles chart on April 4, 1964?

2. True or false: Many women were burned at the stake because they were convicted of witchcraft during the Salem witch trials of 1692.

3. What is the only known sport that is derived from work?

4. In 2002, what were the odds of receiving an A on the average college test or paper in the United States?

5. In 1950, what were the odds of receiving an A on the same?

6. Who was the first athlete to be signed by Nike as an endorser?

7. You mail in an absentee ballot. Then you get hit by a bus and depart this mortal coil. What happens to your vote? Do they throw it out?

REST OF THE QUESTIONS: **1** The Beatles, with (in order) "Can't Buy Me Love," "Twist and Shout," "She Loves You," "I Want to Hold Your Hand," and "Please, Please Me." That week was the only time a single person or group held all the top 5 positions. **2** False. Not a one was burned at the stake. But 150 people were accused and 20 sentenced to death of which 19 were hung and 1 was crushed to death by stones. Those executed numbered 14 women and 6 men. **3** Rodeo. **4** 50% were marked with an A. **5** 20% received an A. **6** Runner Steve Prefontaine in 1974. **7** It gets counted. Votes from people who died *after* voting count. It's the votes from *already dead* people that worry election judges.

This Week in History: November 16, 1959.

The Rodgers and Hammerstein musical *The Sound of Music* opens on Broadway with Mary Martin playing Maria.

YOU *THINK* YOU'RE SO **SMART** !

In the Bible, what color are the 4 horses in the book of Revelation?

TAKE A GUESS

What is the best-selling copyrighted book of all time?

O *Guinness World Records*

O *Dr. Spock's Baby and Child Care*

O *Gone with the Wind*

SO SMART: They are described in Revelation 6:2-8. Pestilence rides a white horse; War rides a red horse; Famine rides a black horse; Death rides a pale green horse.
GUESS: *Guinness World Records* is a clear winner at more than 100 million copies, published in a number of languages and lots of different editions.

TRUE OR FALSE

There are 2 golf balls on the moon.

FOR THE PARTICULARLY BRAINY

If you've lost your rod and reel, but have a rifle, where can you legally go to do a little fishing?

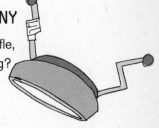

MATCHUPS

Match Rocky Balboa's opponents to the movie each one appeared in:

1. Ivan Drago   A. Rocky III

2. Clubber/Thunderlips   B. Rocky IV

3. Apollo Creed   C. Rocky II

4. Tommy Gunn   D. Rocky

5. Mason Dixon   E. Rocky V

6. Apollo Creed (again) F. Rocky Balboa

T OR F: True. Alan Shepard smuggled aboard 2 golf balls and whacked them with a converted soil sample collector. **BRAINY:** Vermont and Virginia still allow fishing with a rifle. Or is it called hunting? In those states you can shoot at fish, as long as you're on shore and they're underwater. The trick is to aim just in front of the fish and the concussion knocks them unconscious, or kills them outright, and they float to the surface. Hunters (or is that fishermen?), are warned to be careful of bullets that ricochet off objects in the water. **MATCHUPS: 1** B **2** A **3** D **4** E **5** F **6** C.

NOW FOR THE REST
OF THE QUESTIONS

1. What is the average height of a man in the United States?

2. Who in the Bible is made fun of because he was bald?

3. You are in the movie theater with 99 other people. How many out of all of you bought snacks from the concession stand?

4. How many spouses out of 100 keep some extra moolah hidden from their spouses?

5. When was the lawn mower invented?

6. I'm not sure how they found out, but scientists tell us that these two items are the rat's favorite foods. What are they?

7. What percentage of bottled water sold in the United States actually comes straight from the taps of municipal water supplies?

REST OF THE QUESTIONS: **1** 5 feet, 9 inches. **2** Elisha (2 Kings 2:23) **3** Movie experts say that 87% of moviegoers always stop to buy something to nibble on. That's where the Cineplex's profits come from, not from ticket sales. **4** Over 60 have some sort of secret stash of cash. (Hmmm, I wonder where my wife has her stash hidden.) **5** 1830. **6** Scrambled eggs and macaroni and cheese. **7** 25%. Some of the companies filter it 1 more time, but some don't.

This Week in History: November 22, 1927. Carl Eliason of Sayner, Wisconsin, is granted the first patent for a snowmobile design. His first snowmobile is created from parts scavenged from bicycles to a radiator from an old Ford truck.

185

YOU *THINK* YOU'RE SO SMART

In the winter, they put antifreeze in fire hydrants up north so the water doesn't freeze, right?

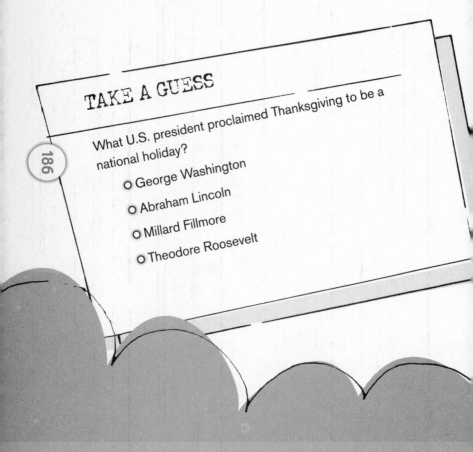

TAKE A GUESS

What U.S. president proclaimed Thanksgiving to be a national holiday?

- O George Washington
- O Abraham Lincoln
- O Millard Fillmore
- O Theodore Roosevelt

SO SMART: No. The reason they don't worry about the water freezing in a hydrant is that there is no water in the hydrant. When a hydrant is closed, the water that is in there automatically drains out and the main water source stays below the level of frozen ground. **GUESS:** Abraham Lincoln in 1863. Although the holiday had its origins in 1621, it took several hundred years for it to catch on.

TRUE OR FALSE

Boa constrictors crush their prey.

FOR THE PARTICULARLY BRAINY

Why are British sailors nicknamed "limeys"?

MATCHUPS

Match the TV dog to the show it appeared on:

1. Pokey

A. *Frazier*

2. Murray

B. *Little House on the Prairie*

3. Eddie

C. *Little Rascals*

4. Bullet

D. *Mad about You*

5. Petey

E. *Roy Rogers*

6. Bandit

F. *Lassie*

NOW FOR THE REST OF THE QUESTIONS

1. How big of a tree did they have to cut down to make this goofy book?

2. All the M&M colors are tasty, but if your favorite color is brown, does the average bag of M&M's give you enough of them?

3. If you're a horse person, what country would you feel most at home in?

4. How much money is lost every hour of every day at Las Vegas casinos?

5. How many puffs do smokers average with each cigarette?

6. How many hotel rooms are there in the United States?

7. How many of these hotel rooms are occupied on any given night?

REST OF THE QUESTIONS: **1** To produce an average-sized paperback, you consume a block of wood that is about the same size as the finished product. **2** It depends, since only 30% of the standard M&M's bag is made up of brown ones. **3** Mongolia. It has the most horses per capita—some figures claim there is 1 horse for every person. **4** The average take in Las Vegas is a few dollars more than $700,000 an hour. Now you know 1 reason they can afford to build such opulent casinos. **5** If you're an average smoker, you get 10 puffs per cigarette. **6** 4.4 million. **7** 2.5 million.

This Week in History: December 2, 1942.
Italian-born Enrico Fermi, Nobel Prize-
winning physicist, directs and controls
the first nuclear chain reaction at the
University of Chicago. That event ushers
in the nuclear age.

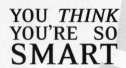

YOU *THINK* YOU'RE SO SMART!

If you want to live to be 100 years old in the United States, you should do this.

TAKE A GUESS

190

What is the ratio of Las Vegas residents to Las Vegas slot machines?

- O 1 for every 14.5 residents
- O 2 for every 10 residents
- O 3 for every 7.5 residents
- O 1 for every 3.5 residents

TRUE OR FALSE

Jesus had a last name, but it is lost to antiquity.

FOR THE PARTICULARLY BRAINY

Who was the only woman to found a major religion?

MATCHUPS

Match the cartoon/animated animal with its TV show/movie/comic strip:

1. Rufus	A. *The Jetsons*
2. Astro	B. *Charlotte's Web*
3. Wilbur	C. *Madeline*
4. Spike	D. *Kim Possible*
5. Genevieve	E. *The Flintstones*
6. Dino	F. *Peanuts*

T OR F: False. Last names were virtually unknown when Jesus was on earth. Surnames did not start appearing until the 10th century, when the Normans conquered England. *Christ* is 1 of the titles given to Jesus. **BRAINY:** Mary Baker Eddy. She founded the Christian Science religion (Church of Christ, Scientist) in 1866. **MATCHUPS: 1** D **2** A **3** B **4** F **5** C **6** E.

NOW FOR THE REST OF THE QUESTIONS

1. Out of 100 Americans, how many believe that aliens have visited the earth?

2. Poll another 100 Americans. How many say they have seen a UFO or know someone who has?

3. Who was the *last* U.S. president who never made it to college?

4. When dining out, what food is ordered the most in the United States?

5. What's number 2 on the dining-out menu?

6. On average, how many times will your darling child nag you to buy them something that you originally refused to purchase?

7. How many whiskers does your average cat have? (No fair counting.)

REST OF THE QUESTIONS: 1 30 of them are believers. **2** 7% of Americans say they have seen a UFO or had a friend or cousin or a friend of a cousin who has seen one. **3** Harry Truman. **4** French fries. **5** What goes with fries? A hamburger, of course. **6** Your average 12- to 17-year-old will nag a parent 9 times until getting it or giving up. **7** The average tabby has 12 on each side of its face.

This Week in History: December 8, 1952.

The first time pregnancy is acknowledged on television in the United States is during the *I Love Lucy* episode, "Lucy Is Enceinte." The word *pregnant* is not allowed to be said on television.

YOU *THINK* YOU'RE SO SMART

What product did chewing gum conglomerate Wrigley begin his business with?

TAKE A GUESS

Ellen Church made aviation history in 1930. What was her claim to fame?

O She was the first U.S. woman pilot.

O She was the first woman to successfully parachute from a plane.

O She was the first stewardess.

SO SMART: Soap. Mr. Wrigley offered a small package of gum as an incentive for customers to buy his soap. People began asking for "just the gum—hold the soap." The rest is history. **GUESS:** In 1930, Ellen Church became the first stewardess on an airplane. Prior to that, airplanes often used small men, called "cabin boys" to help load luggage and aid passengers. Church, a registered nurse, convinced Boeing Air that nurses would be better equipped to handle the frequent air sickness that occurred during those early bumpy flights.

TRUE OR FALSE

Angels have wings.

FOR THE PARTICULARLY BRAINY

Where does Santa Claus need to go if he wants to weigh less?

MATCHUPS

Match the doll to the year it was introduced:

1. Barbie	A. 1960
2. Strawberry Shortcake	B. 1915
3. Bratz	C. 1979
4. Chatty Cathy	D. 1959
5. Cabbage Patch Kids	E. 2001
6. Raggedy Ann	F. 1979

NOW FOR THE REST OF THE QUESTIONS

1. The famous wildlife and bird painter John James Audubon really loved birds and would spend hours observing a species to paint it. True or false?

2. When was the first *professional* sports mascot introduced?

3. In the Bible, who was involved in an all-night wrestling match?

4. If you visit Bethlehem, Pennsylvania, at Christmas, you might see "putzes." What are they?

5. How many people telling a joke laugh more than the people listening to them tell the joke?

6. What's the average cost of a haircut in a U.S. barbershop these days?

7. When did someone invent the shopping cart?

REST OF THE QUESTIONS: **1** False. Because he wanted to paint them as realistically as possible, he shot them and posed them in naturalistic poses. But since dead birds lost color so quickly he shot as many as 100 birds a day for 1 painting. **2** The San Diego Padres Chicken made his debut in 1974. **3** Jacob (Genesis 32:22-31). **4** A type of nativity scene. The name was used by the early Moravian Christians who settled the area in the 1700s. **5** 50% of them. **6** $16 for a man and $21 for a woman. **7** 1937.

This Week in History: December 11, 1972.
Apollo 17 lands on the moon's surface for a
3-day exploration. It is the final U.S. Apollo
mission to the moon.

YOU *THINK* YOU'RE SO SMART!

You're the new owner of an NFL team. You're trying to cut corners because an NFL team costs a lot of money. Hmmm, maybe you can save on footballs. What is the minimum number of footballs you need to have on hand for the first game?

TAKE A GUESS

Will superglue stick to Teflon?

- O yes
- O no
- O maybe

SO SMART: You need to have 36 new footballs 12 are marked with a "K" to be used by the kicker. If you play in an indoor stadium, you are allowed to get by with 24.

GUESS: No. There are no tiny surface cracks for the glue to seep into, so there's no physical bond. For those who think they're smart, no, superglue would not "melt" Teflon to produce a chemical bond either. We're really not sure why anyone would need to know any of this information.

TRUE OR FALSE

Eating turkey makes you sleepy.

FOR THE PARTICULARLY BRAINY

How do most people eat their cake: frosting first or cake first?

MATCHUPS

Match how often the listed incidents happen to hired Santas:

1. Crying children	A. 60%
2. Being wet on	B. 45%
3. Sneezed or coughed on	C. 90%
4. See spots from camera flashes	D. 34%
5. Get their beards pulled	E. 74%

T OR F: True, but only if it is lots and lots of it. Most dieticians say folks overeat at the holidays—and that makes them sleepy. Turkey does contain tryptophan, which does make people nod off, but in order for it to actually work, a person needs to consume a few whole turkeys. **BRAINY:** 70% eat the cake first; 27% eat the frosting first; and 3% eat them together. **MATCHUPS: 1** E **2** D **3** A **4** B **5** C.

NOW FOR THE REST OF THE QUESTIONS

1. What healthy food did Jesus eat after his resurrection to prove he was not a phantom?

2. How much water does your average cow need every day?

3. How many American artists' works hang permanently in the Louvre in Paris?

4. What percentage of U.S. prisoners include an apology in their final words before being executed?

5. How much is the most expensive kindergarten in America?

6. Who was Johnny Carson's most frequent *Tonight Show* guest?

7. What national fast-food chain is closed on Sunday so its employees can go to church?

REST OF THE QUESTIONS: 1 Broiled fish (Luke 24:38-43). **2** Basically, they drink about a bathtub full of water each day or about 50 gallons. Some of it may be in the grass they eat, but still, 50 gallons is 50 gallons. **3** Only 1: James Abbot McNeill Whistler's *Arrangement in Grey and Black, No. 1: The Artist's Mother*. **4** 28% often the crowd a final apology. **5** Brearley School in New York City will set you back a bit over $26,000 a year for your 4-year-old. **6** Bob Hope appeared 132 times. **7** Chick-fil-A, founded by S. Truett Cathy, has always closed on Sundays. The company's corporate purpose says that they exist "to glorify God by being a faithful steward of all that is entrusted to us and to have a positive influence on all who come in contact with Chick-fil-A."

This Week in History: December 17, 1991.

A long meeting between Soviet president, Mikhail Gorbachev, and president of the Russian Federation, Boris Yeltsin, resolves details for the dissolution of the Soviet Union on or before New Year's Eve.

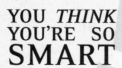

YOU *THINK* YOU'RE SO SMART

In wedding traditions, why is it considered bad luck for the groom to see the bride before the wedding?

TAKE A GUESS

202

What is the percentage of Jews in the entire world population?

- ○ 20%
- ○ 10%
- ○ 2%
- ○ 0.2%

SO SMART: Tradition has it that in an arranged marriage, some grooms saw their intended bride early, did not like what they saw, and took off for parts unknown. If a father were careful, he made sure that no husband-to-be would get an early peek and be spooked off. **GUESS:** Only 0.2% of the world's population is Jewish.

TRUE OR FALSE

Dry ice melts.

FOR THE PARTICULARLY BRAINY

If you have 100 monkeys typing long enough, odds are that they will eventually finish a Shakespearean-length play.

MATCHUPS

Match the robot/android with its TV/movie home:

1. Gort   A. *Short Circuit*

2. Johnny 5   B. *Jimmy Neutron*

3. Rosie the Maid   C. *Lost in Space*

4. C-3PO/R2-D2   D. *The Day the Earth Stood Still*

5. Goddard   E. *The Jetsons*

6. B-9 Robot   F. *Star Wars Episode IV* (first introduced)

T OR F: False. It sublimates, skipping the liquid form. **BRAINY:** Well, maybe. According to a recent computer study, you have to start with a million monkeys, have them type 1 keystroke per second for a full year with no sleep—that will produce 31,000,000 keystrokes a year. But wait, there's more! You would have to give the monkey typists a million years for the project, and then multiply *that* amount of time and energy by 200. So, yes, it could happen, but boy, you would have to have a lot of time, monkeys, and typewriters to get it done. **MATCHUPS: 1** D **2** A **3** E **4** F **5** B **6** C.

NOW FOR THE REST OF THE QUESTIONS

1. When Elvis passed away, how many people made a living pretending to be Elvis?

2. In 2004, how many Elvis impersonators attended the most recent convention for Elvis impersonators?

3. In what country would you find the highest consumption of tea?

4. What is the only Wonder of the Ancient World still standing?

5. What ruler imposed a tax in Jesus' day?

6. Where is the largest clock in the world?

7. How many times can you recycle paper?

REST OF THE QUESTIONS: 1 No more than 50 people were doing Elvis impersonations. **2** 35,000 of the sequined imposters made the trek. **3** Turkey leads the pack with over 1,200 cups of tea consumed per person per year. **4** The Great Pyramid of Giza, Egypt. **5** Caesar (Matthew 22:17-22). **6** The tallest and most visible clock is Big Ben in London at 320 feet high. **7** Only 3 or 4 times. After a while, the paper fibers lose their ability to bind together, resulting in a very weak paper.

This Week in History: December 28, 1945.

The U.S. Pledge of Allegiance is officially

recognized by Congress.

YOU *THINK* YOU'RE SO SMART **!**

What's the average age for a bridegroom in the United States?

TAKE A GUESS

When does a bird's bill become a beak?

○ At 5mm

○ At 7mm

○ At 9mm

SO SMART: 26.8 years old. **GUESS:** A trick question. None of the answers are correct. There is no difference at all between a bill and a beak. However, bird experts seem to prefer the use of the term *bill*.

TRUE OR FALSE

By the 1800s gorillas were common in European zoos.

FOR THE PARTICULARLY BRAINY

What percentage of *all* U.S. purchases are made by women?

MATCHUPS

Match up the partners in these fictional duos:

207

1. Bert	A. Elwood
2. Boris	B. Scully
3. Dangermouse	C. Hutch
4. Jake	D. Natasha
5. Mulder	E. Penfold
6. Starsky	F. Ernie

NOW FOR THE REST OF THE QUESTIONS

1. What is the most common noncontagious disease?

2. Nearly 200,000 books are published every year in the United States. What percentage of Americans think they can write a book?

3. Is it true that there are no 2 snowflakes alike?

4. The lowest U.S. zip code number is 00001.

5. What percentage of people considers themselves lucky? How about those who consider themselves unlucky?

6. Name the only nonelectric musical instrument invented in the 20th century?

7. In 1995, 60% of all purchases were made in cash. What was the percentage 10 years later?

208

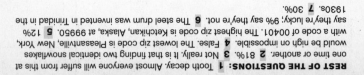

REST OF THE QUESTIONS: 1 Tooth decay. Almost everyone will suffer from this at one time or another. **2** 81%. **3** Not really. It is that finding two identical snowflakes would be nigh on impossible. **4** False. The lowest zip code is Pleasantville, New York, with a code of 00401. The highest zip code is Ketchikan, Alaska, at 99950. **5** 12% say they're lucky; 9% say they're not. **6** The steel drum was invented in Trinidad in the 1930s. **7** 30%.

CONGRATULATIONS on making it almost the whole way through this book. Now don't you feel better for being more smarter than when you started?

Allow me now to completely change the subject.

I seldom get invited to showers.

No . . . I take that back. I NEVER get invited to showers.

Which is a good thing, because when my wife describes the odd and embarrassing games that guests are forced to play at showers, I am most relieved to be absent from the guest list.

But if I were ever invited to a shower or were hosting some other party, the following pages are the sort of quizzes and puzzles I would not hate being asked to do.

Well, I still wouldn't like it—I mean, who wants to work at a party?—but the following trivia-based quizzes are actually kind of fun.

Fun if you're smart, like me.

Not so fun if you are otherwise endowed.

Anyhow, if you need another person to bring a present to your shower . . . I'm busy that day.

By the way, you can make as many copies of the quiz pages as you need for your friends. But keep the answers to yourself.

Have fun!

53 NEW**BABY!**

1. Why are babies so adorable-looking when they are asleep?

- O They look like angels.
- O They're not crying.
- O They're still enough for you to notice.
- O They look just like you.

2. In the United States, the ratio of boy babies to girl babies is

- O 105 boys to 100 girls
- O 105 girls to 100 boys
- O 99 boys to 101 girls

3. You don't plan on it with your children, but how many adults claim that their parents played favorites?

- O 50%
- O 62%
- O 74%
- O 85%

4. How many babies are born each day, on average, in the United States?

- O 9,998
- O 10,001
- O 11,213
- O 13,432

5. In the United States, what's the average age of a first-time mother?

- O 22 years, 8 months
- O 23 years, 2 months
- O 25 years, 1 month
- O 27 years, 4 months

You Think You're So Smart

6. **What was the most popular name for a boy in 2006?**

- O Jack
- O Joshua
- O Caleb
- O Nate

7. **What was the most popular name for a girl in 2006?**

- O Emily
- O Sarah
- O Jessica
- O Erika

8. **How long does a normal baby cry every day?**

- O 1 and 1/2 hours total
- O 2 hours total
- O 2 hours, 20 minutes total
- O 3 hours, 15 minutes total

9. **When surveyed, what percentage of new mothers were grateful their husbands stayed out of the way?**

- O 21%
- O 25%
- O 33%
- O 42%

10. **Out of the 1st 23 NASA astronauts, how many were first-borns?**

- O 14
- O 17
- O 21
- O 22

ANSWERS ON PAGE 235

1. **How many birthday cards can most Americans expect on their birthday?**
   - O 5 cards
   - O 8 cards
   - O 10 cards
   - O 11 cards

2. **On average, how many birthday presents will you receive?**
   - O 1 gift
   - O 3 gifts
   - O 4 gifts
   - O 6 gifts

3. **This month has the fewest birthday babies.**
   - O January
   - O February
   - O September
   - O November

4. **This month has the most birthday babies.**
   - O March
   - O May
   - O June
   - O August

5. **How many free birthday meals did Denny's restaurants cook up during the years they offered it?**
   - O 10 million
   - O 15 million
   - O 22 million
   - O 1.2 billion

6. **In the Bible, who had the first birthday party?**

   O Abraham
   O Moses
   O Joseph
   O Pharaoh

7. **What are your odds of living to 116 or older?**

   O 1 in 50 million
   O 1 in a million
   O 1 in 2 billion
   O 1 in 4 billion

8. **What parts of your body get bigger with age?**

   O Feet, nose, earlobes
   O Feet, hips, tummy
   O Feet, hands, nose
   O Feet, tummy, nose

9. **If you live to be 110, how many other people in the United States are your age?**

   O 35
   O 43
   O 50
   O 61

10. **What U.S. state has the oldest median age? What state has the youngest?**

    O Arizona and California
    O Florida and Utah
    O New York and California
    O New Mexico and Florida

ANSWERS ON PAGE 235

55 BLUSHING**BRIDE!**

1. You've just been given the biggest diamond ever found in the world. How many carats is it?
   - O 147 carats
   - O 1,100 carats
   - O 2,500 carats
   - O 3,106 carats

2. At a wedding, how many jars of water did Jesus miraculously turn into wine?
   - O 3
   - O 6
   - O 7
   - O 12

3. What was the average cost of a wedding in 2004?
   - O $18,575
   - O $20,000
   - O $23,000
   - O $26,000

4. What's the average number of guests a U.S. bride will invite to her big day?
   - O 100
   - O 125
   - O 150
   - O 175

5. How many people fail to RSVP?
   - O 10%
   - O 12%
   - O 25%
   - O 30%

6. Out of 100 American brides surveyed, how many cried at their wedding?

O 45
O 50
O 65
O 85

7. Out of 100 American grooms surveyed, how many cried at their wedding?

O 15
O 25
O 30
O 35

8. What's the average price of a U.S. bride-to-be's gown?

O $800
O $1,000
O $1,050
O $1,200

9. In 1981, what did 4,000 Brits a day pay about $3.00 (U.S.) to see?

O Princess Di's wedding dress
O Princess Di's royal wedding coach
O The 1,200 royal wedding gifts
O Prince Charles and Princess Di's honeymoon suite

10. What percentage of 70-year-olds says to their spouses, "You get more attractive to me every day"?

O 33%
O 40%
O 50%
O 60%

ANSWERS ON PAGE 235

1. What is the English translation of the New Year's celebratory song title *Auld Lang Syne*?

- O Long time ago
- O Longer than you know
- O Old long ago
- O Older than the sun

2. What is the oldest holiday celebrated by mankind?

- O Samhain
- O New Year's Day
- O May Day
- O All Souls' Day

3. Who is responsible for choosing January 1st as the 1st day of the new year?

- O Plato
- O Julius Caesar
- O Pope Gregory
- O Thomas Aquinas

4. Western society's calendar was generated from what?

- O The Druids' calendar
- O Ptolemaic calculations
- O The Gregorian calendar
- O Leonardo da Vinci's daily planner

5. Where does the name *January* come from?

- O Janus
- O Janvier
- O Junius
- O Jansenism

You Think You're So Smart

6. Who uses animals to mark years?

- O Astrologers
- O Astronomers
- O Native American tribes
- O Chinese

7. What parade on New Year's Day tops all parades for television viewing?

- O Tournament of Roses Parade
- O Mardi Gras
- O Macy's Parade
- O Cirque du Soleil Parade

8. Okay, after every year's parade, there's a college football game. What followed the parade from 1903 to 1915?

- O A horse race
- O A battle of the college bands
- O A bicycle race
- O A chariot race

9. Before the festivities came to Time's Square, where did New Yorkers ring in the New Year?

- O Coney Island
- O The Empire State Building
- O Trinity Church
- O Central Park

10. How much does it cost to attend the celebration in Times Square?

- O Free
- O $10
- O $25
- O $35

ANSWERS ON PAGE 236

57 SWEET**RETIREMENT!**

1. **What was the minimum wage when it was introduced in 1938?**
   - ○ 16¢ an hour
   - ○ 19¢ an hour
   - ○ 25¢ an hour
   - ○ 27¢ an hour

2. **How many workdays does it take just to pay your average taxes?**
   - ○ About 90 days
   - ○ About 100 days
   - ○ About 120 days
   - ○ About 130 days

3. **When surveyed, what percentage of American workers said they would rather have a man for a boss?**
   - ○ 40%
   - ○ 43%
   - ○ 45%
   - ○ 48%

4. **On average, how many jobs has the 39-year-old U.S. worker had?**
   - ○ 5
   - ○ 6
   - ○ 7
   - ○ 9

5. **Crazy bosses notwithstanding, what's the #1 complaint of employees?**
   - ○ The office is too cold.
   - ○ The office is too warm.
   - ○ The pay is too low.
   - ○ We have to work too many hours.

6. On average, out of a 40-hour work week, how many hours are spent in meetings?

O 6 hours
O 8 hours
O 10 hours
O 12 hours

7. How many workers have been asked to lie for their boss?

O 45%
O 50%
O 60%
O 90%

8. With part of your retirement funds, you bought 10 Picasso paintings. How many, statistically speaking, are fakes?

O 4
O 5
O 8
O 9

9. You arrive at work happy but leave unhappy because your work was criticized by the boss. What are the chances of that happening?

O 1 chance in 3
O 1 chance in 5
O 1 chance in 7
O 1 chance in 10

10. What is the increase in risk of suffering a heart attack after being fired?

O 75%
O 80%
O 85%
O 100%

ANSWERS ON PAGE 236

58 GOBBLIN' GOOD!

1. **Every year who presents a live turkey to the president of the United States?**
   - ○ The vice president
   - ○ Butterball Farms
   - ○ National Wild Turkey Federation
   - ○ Wild Turkey Shoot Federation

2. **What bird did Benjamin Franklin want as the nation's official bird?**
   - ○ The turkey
   - ○ The golden eagle
   - ○ The pheasant
   - ○ The red-tailed hawk

3. **What year did Macy's Parade make its Thanksgiving Day debut?**
   - ○ 1920
   - ○ 1924
   - ○ 1930
   - ○ 1932

4. **What percentage of Americans will eat turkey on Thanksgiving?**
   - ○ 65%
   - ○ 75%
   - ○ 80%
   - ○ 91%

5. **What country eats the most turkey per capita?**
   - ○ The United States
   - ○ Canada
   - ○ Israel
   - ○ Australia

6. **Name 1 place where turkey has been eaten only once.**

   ○ Mt. Everest
   ○ The moon
   ○ The South Pole
   ○ The North Pole

7. **How many turkeys are raised in the United States each year?**

   ○ 200 million
   ○ 300 million
   ○ 350 million
   ○ 400 million

8. **How much does the average Thanksgiving Day meal cost?**

   ○ $45
   ○ $48
   ○ $55
   ○ $60

9. **What did the pilgrims wear on their shoes and hats?**

   ○ Dried turkey wishbones
   ○ Buckles
   ○ Bows
   ○ None of the above

10. **I'm not sure who eats them, but they come with the bird—what are giblets, exactly?**

    ○ Soft bones
    ○ Edible offal
    ○ Turkey fat
    ○ Turkey unmentionables

ANSWERS ON PAGE 237

59 CHRISTMAS**SPIRIT!**

1. Write the names of Santa's reindeer.

_____

_____

_____

_____

_____

_____

_____

2. How many U.S. homes would Santa visit on Christmas Eve if you eliminated the "bah humbugs" and naughty children?

○ 100,000,000 homes
○ 200,000,000 homes
○ 250,000,000 homes
○ 300,000,000 homes

3. What is the most frequently recorded Christmas song of all time?

○ "White Christmas"
○ "Feliz Navidad"
○ "Little Drummer Boy"
○ "Have Yourself a Merry Little Christmas"

4. How much does the average American spend on Christmas gifts?

○ $250
○ $300
○ $500
○ $750

You Think You're So Smart

5. **If you look at all the Santas in the mall, what would you guess their average weight is?**
   - O 185 lbs.
   - O 220 lbs.
   - O 240 lbs.
   - O 260 lbs.

6. **When was the first Christmas card sent?**
   - O 1834
   - O 1840
   - O 1843
   - O 1854

7. **Your child's letter to Santa Claus will be delivered to a post office in . . .**
   - O The North Pole
   - O Tahiti
   - O Juneau, Alaska
   - O Santa Claus, Indiana

8. **According to the Bible, how many wise men came to Bethlehem?**
   - O 3
   - O 4
   - O 5
   - O It doesn't say.

9. **How many pet owners will buy their pet a Christmas present?**
   - O 25%
   - O 50%
   - O 55%
   - O 90%

10. **In 2006, how much was the most expensive pet Christmas present offered by regular retailers?**
    - O A $175 cashmere polo shirt
    - O A $245 cashmere sweater-vest
    - O A $250 gold-and-crystal food bowl
    - O All of the above

ANSWERS ON PAGE 237

1. **What country has the longest national anthem?**

   O Greece
   O Morocco
   O Italy
   O United States

2. **What country has the shortest national anthem?**

   O Japan and Jordan
   O Trinidad and Tobago
   O England and France

3. **If you can't sing, what country's national anthem is perfect for you?**

   O Ecuador
   O China
   O Bahrain

4. **Scrabble experts say these 6 letters could score a "bingo" for you.**

   O S-A-T-I-R-E
   O I-N-S-E-R-T
   O O-A-T-E-R-S
   O R-A-T-I-O-N

5. **What is the average intelligence of the average dog compared to the age of the average child?**

   O 1 year
   O 18 months
   O 2 years
   O 3 years

6. **What is the average intelligence of the average cat compared to the age of the average child?**

- O 6 months
- O 1 year
- O 18 months
- O 2 years

7. **Pick the 1 name that doesn't belong in this list:**

- O Dione
- O Phoebe
- O Miranda
- O Rhea

8. **The well-known bugle call "Retreat," was written during:**

- O the Crimean War
- O the Civil War
- O the Boer War
- O the Crusades

9. **The only pitcher to pitch a perfect game in a World Series (so far) is:**

- O Don Larsen
- O Orel Hershiser
- O Bob Feller
- O Roger Clemens

10. **The character "Mr. Peanut" was created in 1916 by 12-year-old Antonio Gentile in a nationwide contest. How much did Planters lavish on this budding artist?**

- O $1,000
- O peanuts for life
- O $100
- O $5

ANSWERS ON PAGE 238

1. **How many computer owners have seriously considered assaulting their infernal machines?**

   O 28%
   O 34%
   O 40%
   O 60%

2. **How many people have actually beaten their poor computer to a pulp?**

   O 10%
   O 12%
   O 14%
   O 20%

3. **What do the following sports teams have in common?**

   Philadelphia 76ers
   Cleveland Cavaliers
   Buffalo Bills
   Cleveland Browns
   Chicago Cubs

   O They are in northern cities.
   O They are all champions.
   O Each name was chosen from fans' contest entries.
   O They have moved from another city.

4. **In the game of Monopoly, what 3 properties are landed on most often?**

   O Illinois Avenue
   O Go
   O B&O Railroad
   O Park Place

5. **You may live on one. What does the word *cul-de-sac* mean?**

   O quiet place
   O rounded street
   O end of the road
   O bottom of the bag

6. **What is the 1 food that cockroaches won't eat?**

   O Cucumbers
   O Tomatoes
   O Peanut butter
   O Liver

7. **How many days a year, on average, does the sun shine in Los Angeles?**

   O 278
   O 299
   O 329
   O 342

8. **Where does a burglar head to first when burgling a house?**

   O The garage
   O The master bedroom
   O The family room
   O The kitchen

9. **Who was the first mascot for a U.S. sports team?**

   O A goat
   O A horse
   O A bulldog
   O A badger

10. **In 2005, how many Americans claimed they jog?**

   O 14 million
   O 22 million
   O 37 million
   O 48 million

ANSWERS ON PAGE 239

1. Your Uncle Charlie tells you he lived through Hurricane Ursula. But you know he has to be fibbing. Why?

   ○ A name beginning with "U" is never used.
   ○ Uncle Charlie doesn't live in hurricane country.
   ○ Hurricane names are never exotic names.
   ○ He really meant to say a tornado called Ursula.

2. In 2010, a weatherman says that Hurricane Andrew is forming off Miami. You phone the station and challenge the forecast. Why?

   ○ Hurricanes form farther out in the ocean.
   ○ Hurricane names are never repeated.
   ○ The names of violent hurricanes are retired.
   ○ The hurricane isn't formed enough to be named.

3. On average, how long does it take most Americans to fall asleep?

   ○ 9 minutes
   ○ 11 minutes
   ○ 13 minutes
   ○ 15 minutes

4. How much did the Speedo version of a 1900s bathing suit weigh?

   ○ 0
   ○ 8 oz.
   ○ 12 oz.
   ○ 2 lbs.

5. How many government documents are labeled "classified"?

   O 850,000
   O 4 million
   O 10 million
   O 14 million

6. Plop 100 Americans in front of a TV tuned to the Weather Channel. How many will not move for the next 3 hours?

   O 15 of them
   O 20 of them
   O 25 of them
   O 38 of them

7. For weather predictions, how often is the *Old Farmer's Almanac* correct?

   O 24%
   O 51%
   O 60%
   O 75%

8. Which of your legs weighs more—the right or the left?

   O The right
   O The left
   O They weigh the same.

9. Who is the most mentioned man in the Bible?

   O Moses
   O Jesus
   O Peter
   O John

10. How old do you have to be in order to start smiling?

   O 6 weeks old
   O 7 weeks old
   O 8 weeks old
   O 10 weeks old

ANSWERS ON PAGE 239

63 PARTY**TIME!**

1. **Which vehicle gets the best gas mileage?**

   O Moped, using the motor

   O *Saturn V* rocket with capsule

   O Honda Civic

   O A supertanker carrying crude oil

2. **Number these 8 animals in order of intelligence (1 being the smartest).**

   ____Dog

   ____Pig

   ____Horse

   ____Cat

   ____Cow

   ____Sheep

   ____Chicken

   ____Turkey

3. **Complete the following sequence: M, Y, X, Y, Z, P, T, L,?**

   O A

   O K

   O R

   O Q

4. **Sir Isaac Newton was twice elected to the British Parliament. What is he remembered for?**

   O His passionate speeches

   O His attention to legal details

   O His loyalty to the Crown

   O None of the options

5. **You are on death row, the morning of your execution. What will be the last thing you want to eat? (rank in order of requests)**

   ____French fries

   ____Hamburger

   ____Steak

   ____Ice cream

   ____Fried chicken

You Think You're So Smart

6. Who was 53310761?

- ○ G. Gordon Liddy
- ○ The Birdman of Alcatraz
- ○ Elvis Presley
- ○ Lee Harvey Oswald

---

7. *Deft*, *first*, and *laughing* all share a common characteristic. What word from the list to the right also qualifies?

- ○ spaghetti
- ○ larynx
- ○ violin
- ○ canopy
- ○ shirtsleeve

---

8. What is the most popular last name in the English language?

- ○ Jones
- ○ Miller
- ○ Smith
- ○ Johnson

---

9. Here are the 5 most frequently used letters of the alphabet. Rank them in order.

____E

____A

____T

____N

____O

---

10. Write the plural of Mrs.

_____

ANSWERS ON PAGE 240

1. **Which rich person never used preprinted checks?**
   - O Cornelius Vanderbilt
   - O Andrew Carnegie
   - O Howard Hughes
   - O J. D. Rockefeller

2. **Pick the one that doesn't belong:**
   - O cellophane
   - O zipper
   - O nylon
   - O xylophone

3. **The word *ukulele* comes from the Hawaiian word for:**
   - O cat
   - O flea
   - O wind
   - O strum

4. **The most commonly used word(s) in conversation in the English language is:**
   - O ya know
   - O a
   - O I
   - O the

5. **What are the odds that a 70-year-old needs glasses?**
   - O 50%
   - O 66%
   - O 78%
   - O 90%

You Think You're So Smart

6. How did unwanted e-mail get the moniker *spam*?

- O The first "spammer" worked for Hormel.
- O The first e-mail spam was advertising the canned meat.
- O Sending real Spam was suggested as revenge.
- O The culprit was sent to prison where he ate lots of Spam.

7. Do trees die of old age?

- O No
- O Yes
- O Maybe

8. Where did the word *jazz* come from?

- O No one knows for certain
- O From the Arabic word *chasse*
- O From the African word *jaiza*
- O From the Hindu word *jasba*

9. Who are the tallest people in the world, according to their country?

- O Swedes
- O Dutch
- O Norwegians
- O Americans

10. How fast was the first "speeder" in the United States going to get the first speeding ticket?

- O 10 mph
- O 12 mph
- O 25 mph
- O 50 mph

ANSWERS ON PAGE 240

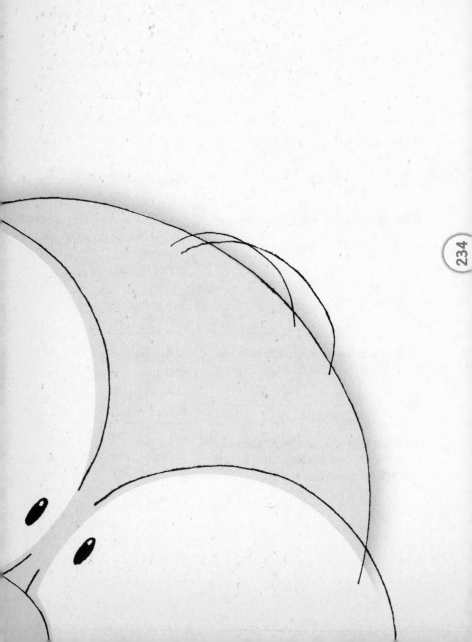

ANSWERS TO THE PARTY QUIZZES

53: NEW BABY!

1 The first two answers are correct. One school of thought states that humans are hardwired, DNA-wise, to be protective of small babies. Something about the infants being helpless and vulnerable when asleep causes the normal human to see them as angelic. The other school of thought states that babies can be really, really troublesome when they are awake, crying and fussing and throwing up, etc. (Just ask a new parent if you're unsure of all the work a new baby entails.) These students of human nature claim that once the baby is quiet and sleeping, our stress levels go way, way down and we can once again see them as angelic. **2** Just about 105 boys to every 100 girls. **3** 85%. **4** 11,213. **5** 25 years, 1 month. **6** Jack, followed by Joshua. **7** Jessica, followed by Emily. **8** 2 hours, 20 minutes. **9** 21%. **10** 21.

54: HAPPY BIRTHDAY!

1 8 cards. **2** 4 gifts. **3** February. In 2004, that was the month with the fewest births. **4** August. If birthdays were distributed evenly, 8.3% of the population would celebrate a birthday each month. But August registers a whopping 9.14%! **5** By the time the program ended in 1993, Denny's had given out 10 million free meals. **6** Pharaoh, at the time Joseph was in Egypt (Genesis 40:20). **7** Only 1 person in 2 billion will live that long. **8** Your feet, your nose, and your earlobes. **9** There are no more than 50 documented 110-year-olds in the world at any one time. **10** Florida is the oldest at nearly 39, compared with the national median age of 35. Utah is the youngest at 27.

55: BLUSHING BRIDE!

1 A diamond weighing in at 3,106 carats was found in South Africa in 1905. It was later cut into 9 different diamonds. **2** 6 (John 2:1-10). **3** The price tag was close to $23,000. **4** 125 guests are invited. We could find no firm figure on how many actually show up, though. **5** Although hopefully the numbers are better for wedding invitations, more than 30% of invitees to events asking for an RSVP didn't bother answering. **6** 45 of them shed tears at some point during the ceremony. **7** 25 of them shed manly tears. **8** $800. **9** The 1,200 wedding gifts the royal couple received. **10** 60%.

56: NEW YEAR COUNTDOWN!

1 "Old long ago." The Scottish song was written primarily by Robert Burns, but wasn't published until 1796, well after his death. **2** The correct answer is—check the category!—New Year's Day (I made up Samhain). New Year's Day was first observed by the Babylonians about 4,000 years ago. They celebrated in March—the beginning of spring—and the celebrations lasted for more than a week. **3** Julius Caesar. In 153 BC, the Roman senate voted to make January 1 the 1st day of the new year, but over the years, Roman emperors kept tampering with the calendar. It wasn't until 46 BC that Julius Caesar officially established the 1st day of January as the 1st official day of the year. But . . . he had to make 1 year 445 days long to get the calendar back in sync with the sun. **4** The Gregorian calendar. **5** The Roman god Janus—who was known as the god of beginnings and the gatekeeper of doors and entrances. He was known to have the ability to look backwards and forwards at the same time. **6** The Chinese. Based on a 12-year cycle, the Chinese believe that people born in a specific year carry the traits of the animals represented. The animals include a boar, a dog, a dragon, a rabbit, a horse, a tiger, a sheep, a snake, a rat, an ox, a monkey, and a rooster. **7** Without question, the Tournament of Roses Parade in Pasadena, California. It has been a tradition since 1890. **8** For those years, the parade was followed by Roman-style chariot races. Really. **9** Trinity Church was the favorite spot between the years of 1890 and 1904—although the celebration was less raucous than the Times Square event. **10** It has always been free. If you plan on attending, officials say to get there early so you can actually see the ball drop—and dress warmly. It is New York, after all.

57: SWEET RETIREMENT!

1 25¢ an hour. **2** A little more than 100 days, working to support all forms of government. **3** 48%. **4** 9. **5** The office is too cold. **6** 10 hours. **7** More than 90% of Americans say their boss asked them to fib for them. Things like "Tell them I'm at lunch . . . or in a meeting!" when they really weren't. **8** Probably 4 of them are fake. Experts say that between 10 and 40% of art sold in galleries are fakes. The best-known artists are most likely to be forged since there's more money in a painting by "Picasso" than in a painting of

Elvis on black velvet. Forgers claim that most modern art is easier to duplicate than the old masters. **9** 1 chance in 5. **10** The risk goes up 100%; for the managers who do the firing, the risk doubles.

58: GOBBLIN' GOOD!

1 The National Wild Turkey Federation. For more than 50 years, the NWTF has given the president a live turkey and 2 dressed turkeys in celebration of Thanksgiving. Harry Truman was the first to get the turkeys. Each year, the president "pardons" the live turkey who goes off to an historical farm to live out the rest of its years. It's a very thankful turkey. **2** Ben lobbied for the turkey, proclaiming: "O [I] wish the eagle had not been chosen as the representative of our country. The turkey is a much more respectable bird and a true original native of America." **3** 1924. More than 1,000 employees took part in the 5-mile parade—originally called Macy's Christmas Parade. Today, the route has been shortened to 2.5 miles, and millions watch on television as the giant balloons are marched down the street. **4** The turkey people say that more than 91% of Americans will have turkey at their meal that day. **5** Israel eats the most at nearly 28 pounds of turkey per person per year. The United States is second at 18 pounds. **6** The moon. When Neil Armstrong and Buzz Aldrin sat down to eat their first meal on the moon, their foil food packets contained roasted turkey and all the trimmings. **7** 300 million. **8** A basic traditional meal for 10 people costs a little over $45 (but not with my family). That meal consists of turkey, sweet potatoes, peas, rolls, and pumpkin pie. Cool Whip costs extra. **9** None of the answers. If you guessed "buckles," they did not come into fashion until nearly a century later. You can blame the misconception on advertising and old children's picture books. **10** Giblets are the edible offal of a fowl, typically including the heart, gizzard, liver, and other visceral organs. The term is culinary usage only; zoologists do not refer to the "giblets" of a bird.

59: CHRISTMAS SPIRIT!

1 In Clement Moore's 1823 poem, "A Visit from St. Nicholas," the reindeer named were: Dasher, Dancer, Prancer, Vixen, Comet, Cupid, Donder, and Blitzen. *Donder* is the German word for *thunder*; *Blitzen* is the word for *lightning*. And, yes, someone is missing—Rudolph. He's not part of the original authorized list but, hey, he's the most famous. **2** 200,000,000 homes, give or take a few homes where a child has been reevaluated from nice to naughty. **3** "White Christmas," written by Irving Berlin in 1942, tops the Christmas recordings. **4** $750 (or so they say). **5** 220 lbs. **6** 1843. **7** Santa Claus, Indiana, is the official destination for all those wish lists addressed to Santa. **8** It doesn't say. We say there are 3 because they brought 3 gifts. But the Bible just says wise men from the East. Some say there might have been 100 people or more in the party, and they could have traveled from as far away as Korea. **9** Surveys indicate that 55% of owners will buy a special Christmas present for their pet. **10** All of the pet presents listed were carried by Neiman Marcus who had the most expensive gifts I could find in regular retail. Extravagant, but not the top of the market. According to petgadgets.com, Cincinnati Bengals' quarterback Carson Palmer's 3 dogs are getting a 50 square-foot $25,000 mansion, complete with a mahogany hand-crafted front door, 7-foot ceilings, slate floors, air conditioning, designer furnishings, a plasma TV, and DVD players. Oh, and for that same $25,000 you can buy the Pet Spa, which automatically bathes and dries your dog in 25 minutes. Also available: A $4,000 pink glitter pet carrier from the movie *Legally Blonde*; a $24,000 Louis the 15th-style rosewood pet bed; a $1,000 quilted metallic Italian lambskin coat; French perfume for dogs at $3,000 a bottle; a $895 CinePetLounger, a pooch bed complete with a popcorn bowl for snacking when watching the big game; and finally, a $19,000 9-carat diamond necklace from the Pet's Jeweler. (I looked up the Pet's Jeweler on the Web. They call themselves the "jeweler to the stars . . . understated, elegant, unique, and always very chic.")

60: PARTY TIME!

1 Take a deep breath—the Greek national anthem contains 158 verses! **2** Breathe easier—Japan's and Jordan's national anthems each are 4 lines long. **3** Bahrain's national anthem is a music-only song—no words at all. **4** Scrabble scholars agree that the letters S-A-T-I-R-E lend themselves to more combinations than any other 6 letters. A "bingo" is using all 7 letters you are holding in 1 turn to score a 50-point bonus. **5** The average dog's smart quotient is equivalent to a 2-year-old child. **6** Experts claim that the average feline's smarts is equivalent to an 18-month-old child. (Hmmm, are the dog experts weighing in on this one?) **7** Astronomers will know this one—Miranda is the odd one out because it is a moon of Uranus. The others listed are moons of Saturn. **8** The song has truly ancient origins. It is one of the few bugle calls known to have been used by the medieval Crusaders. **9** The Yankees' Don Larsen accomplished this singular feat in the 5th game of the 1956 World Series against the Brooklyn Dodgers. **10** $5.

61: PARTY TIME!

1 Over 40% of us have given the subject some serious thought. **2** Nearly 10% have done bodily harm to their computers. **3** They were all named in contests—as were the Milwaukee Bucks, San Jose Sharks, and Seattle Mariners (if you named them, too). **4** Illinois Avenue, Go, B&O Railroad—in that order. **5** The word is literally translated "bottom of the bag." **6** Cockroach experts say that the little creatures do not fancy cucumbers. **7** 329—that's why they need those fashionable sunglasses. **8** The master bedroom. **9** In 1892, a Yale student paid $5 for a bulldog, calling him Handsome Dan. He barked menacingly at opponents and was thought to bring the Yalies luck—so he stayed as a permanent fixture. The original bulldog, upon his demise, was stuffed and placed in a trophy case in the school's gym. **10** 37 million.

62: PARTY TIME!

1 Because the national hurricane people who name hurricanes never use the letters Q, U, X, Y, and Z—too few names begin with those letters. **2** Whenever a hurricane is particularly violent, the name is retired out of sensitivity to the victims. There will be no Andrew Jr, or Katrina II. **3** 15 minutes. **4** Technically, 0 because Speedos were nonexistent back then, of course. Bathing suits were made of wool. When wet, a woman's suit could weigh as much as 20 lbs. **5** 14 million. **6** 20 of them. **7** Publishers claim about 60% accuracy, but their predictions are fairly generalized. **8** On the average American adult male the right leg weighs 625 grams and the left leg weighs 600 grams. **9** Jesus. **10** When a baby reaches 8 weeks of age they will smile deliberately for the first time.

63: PARTY TIME!

1 Cornelius Vanderbilt wrote out his checks on a half sheet of regular writing paper. Was that legal? Actually, a check can be written on nearly anything and in pencil if you prefer. But I'd double-check with your banking institution if you plan to do this on a regular basis. **2** Xylophone. All the other names were, at one time, brand names for commercial products which have since entered the language as generic terms. **3** Flea—but no one knows quite why. **4** The most frequently spoken word is *I*. The most common written word is *the*, followed by *of* and *and*. **5** Virtually all of them do. Over 9 out of 10 require some sort of vision enhancement. **6** It started on April 12, 1994. An attorney in Phoenix sent out an unsolicited e-mail to thousands of people on several online message boards. An anonymous poster suggested that everyone who was upset should send "coconuts and Spam" to the offending lawyer. Coconuts did not seem to resonate, but Spam sure did, much to the delight of all those Hormel employees in Austin, Minnesota. **7** Not in the sense that people do. Humans have a fixed life span, give or take a few years. But not so with trees. Fires, disease, and insects kill most trees. There is a species called the bristlecone pine that lives between 200 and 400 years. But a few are more than 4,000 years old. **8** Actually, all of the answers are correct to a certain degree. No one knows for certain, but the following languages have all taken partial credit for it. The Arabs claim it's from the word *chasse*, a dance step, as well as the word *jazib* which means "one who allures." The Africans say it comes from their word *jaiza* meaning "the sound of distant drums" and the Hindus believe its root is from the word *jasba* meaning "ardent desire." **9** It used to be Americans, but now, on average, Swedes are 1/2-inch taller and the Dutch and Norwegians are 1 inch taller than us. **10** In 1899, the driver had zoomed 12 miles per hour in an 8-miles-per-hour zone.

64: PARTY TIME!

1 The rocket, man. The rocket spends a lot of energy getting going, then practically coasts the whole way, getting around 300 miles to the gallon. The moped gets 120 miles per gallon, the tanker gets 31 feet to the gallon, and the Honda gets 45 miles to the gallon. **2** The original list is in the correct order. **3** The correct letter is K. Readers of *Superman* comics will recognize the name Mr. Myxyzptlk. Superman had to get the little imp to say his name backwards to get him back to whence he came. **4** Well, one speech, that we know of, or at least the only one recorded. Sir Newton's speech was short, sweet, and to the point: "Would someone please open a window?" **5** The list is in the correct order of most requested. **6** Elvis Presley. It was not his number in *Jailhouse Rock*, but his U.S. Army serial number. **7** *Canopy* is the only word on the list that contains 3 consecutive letters in alphabetical order—nop—just like the others. Other words that are members of the club are *calmness*, *stupid*, and *hijack*. **8** Smith tops the list. The rest of the list, in descending order, is Jones, Johnson, Williams, Brown, Miller, David, Anderson, Wilson, and Thompson. **9** The correct order of most frequent usage is E, T, O, A, and N. **10** Mrs.

Afterword

If you want to learn more about the author (though we can't imagine why anyone would want to do that) or if you want to challenge a specific bit of trivia in this book (*that* we could imagine), visit his wonderfully inadequate Web site: www.jimkraus.com. If you think you have more trivial trivia than that of the trivial author, we (the *royal* we, of course) encourage you to submit it at this site.

If you, the book-buying public, purchases . . . like a million copies of this book, the publishers will have to ask the author to do another book just like the first one—thus confirming the Law of the Successful Sequel. And if that happens, said trivial author possibly might use your trivia and give you a credit line . . . in very teeny, tiny type . . . but a credit nonetheless.

JIM KRAUS is a 1972 graduate of the University of Pittsburgh, with a degree in English and Communication. He attended the Paris-American Academy in France where he learned to effectively point at various menu selections, as well as get lost on the Metro without even trying. Jim has been a journalist for a small-town newspaper in southern Minnesota, has worked in sales, and was an editor for a trade magazine. For the last 15 years, he has been a senior vice president at Tyndale House Publishers. A collector at heart, Jim is happily buried in a snowglobe collection (250) and also enjoys his 300 miniature souvenir buildings (the Statue of Liberty with an illuminated torch is his favorite). "I love collecting things that I can buy in tacky airport gift shops." Jim and his wife have written 10 books together in addition to Jim's 5 solo efforts. The Kraus clan includes Jim, his wife, their 4th-grade son, and a sweet miniature schnauzer, Rufus, who are all allowed to coexist with their ill-tempered cat, P. D., in the Midwest.